Aye or Nae

The Referendum Experience in Scotland 1979-2014

Aye or Nae

The Referendum Experience in Scotland 1979-2014

Peter Lynch

welsh academic press

Cardiff

Published in Wales by Welsh Academic Press, an imprint of

Ashley Drake Publishing Ltd
PO Box 733
Cardiff
CF14 7ZY

www.welsh-academic-press.wales

First Impression – 2019

ISBN
978-1-86057-140-4

British Library Cataloguing-in-Publication Data.
A CIP catalogue for this book is available from the British Library.

Typeset by Prepress Plus, India (www.prepressplus.in)

Contents

In memory of Alasdair Ross

Introduction

At 8.20am on Friday the 24th June 2016, David Cameron walked out into Downing Street to announce his resignation as Prime Minister of the United Kingdom. The resignation followed Cameron's defeat at the referendum on continued membership of the European Union on 23rd June. Political reality required Prime Minister Cameron to leave office with his authority completely undermined by the failed referendum gamble. When he became Conservative leader in 2005, he had criticised his own party for always 'banging on about Europe' rather than the real issues voters cared about. He had used various positions and policies to try to manage the EU issue – moving Conservatives out of the Christian Democrat group in the European Parliament, legislation to trigger a referendum to protect UK sovereignty, various changes to immigration rules and a pre-referendum renegotiation of membership similar to Labour Prime Minister Harold Wilson in 1975. However, the result was a victory for Leave, which won 51.9 per cent (17,410,742 votes) as against 48.1 per cent for Remain (16,141,241 votes).

Cameron had chosen the referendum for reasons of internal party management to deal with the large number of Eurosceptic critics in his party (from ordinary members up to cabinet ministers) as well as the external electoral threat of UKIP. Both the Conservative Party and its backbenchers had supported an in-out referendum during the coalition years from 2010-2015, and had published a draft referendum bill for an in-out referendum in 2013 which was given legislative form as a private members bill by Conservative MP James Wharton in 2013 (it became the European Union (Referendum) Bill 2014). Given continued political pressure on Europe and immigration, the proposal became part of the 2015 Conservative election manifesto (Conservative Party 2015). Though the manifesto majored on implementing a long-term economic plan – a constant refrain from Conservatives in advance of the election – the idea of a secure economic future was accompanied by a proposal for an in-out referendum to be held by the end of 2017 (Conservative Party, 2015: 72): a broad time period that moved the issue away from the general election.[1] This initiative was reliant upon a Conservative majority in the election of May 2015 – which was duly delivered – but even then, there was the expectation that the referendum would confirm the UK's position within the European Union, albeit under renegotiated terms of membership. However, exactly the opposite happened, with salutary lessons for the use of referendums to solve party problems as well as the imperfect conduct of referendum campaigns (Electoral Reform Society 2016). This particular referendum and its conduct was one of the reasons for the creation of the Independent Commission on Referendums by the UCL Constitution Unit in August 2017. It set out to examine five particular issues:

- The place that referendums should play in the UK's system of representative democracy
- the legal effect of referendums and whether any additional constitutional safeguards are needed
- the role of government during the campaign
- the regulation of the designated campaign groups
- the provision of public information and education, and promotion of informed debate.

The 2016 referendum did not just deliver a clear vote for the UK's exit from the European Union – and a legal muddle on procedure that went all the way to the UK Supreme Court - it also brought with it significant earthquakes and aftershocks. In short, it was not a containable political event – it had serious political and economic consequences in the short and long terms. It did unleash the very demons that Prime Minister Cameron had feared in advance (Oliver 2017). Politically, the result triggered an immediate Conservative leadership contest and the withdrawal of prominent Leave campaigner Boris Johnson from the race amongst serious intra-party conflict following the referendum. Very quickly, the leadership race became a procession – as contestants withdrew from the race as MPs voted to produce a shortlist of two - and Theresa May was then installed as Prime Minister on 13th July 2016 without the contest facing a ballot of the party membership. Labour leader Jeremy Corbyn also came under severe pressure to resign following on from the Brexit vote, as his MPs attempted to launch a parliamentary coup against him, using the pretext of the failed referendum campaign. Labour MPs passed a vote of no confidence in Corbyn by 172 to 40 and most of his shadow cabinet resigned at regular intervals in the days following the EU referendum. There followed weeks of speculation about the rules and regulations of any leadership contest – whether Corbyn could stand without being nominated by 50 MPs and MEPs and whether new members could vote in the leadership ballot. Legal action followed in several directions. He remained in office but was then challenged as leader by Labour MP Owen Smith. Corbyn won the leadership election by 61.8 per cent to Smith's 38.2 per cent on 24th September and then set about constructing a new shadow cabinet and attempted to deal with the Brexit issue through more nuanced positions at and beyond the 2017 general election in recognition of the popularity of the Leave option amongst actual and potential Labour voters.

Finally, UKIP leader Nigel Farage announced he would stand down as he had effectively accomplished his political goal but UKIP then entered a fractious leadership contest, assisted by one of the favourites – Steven Woolfe MEP - being excluded from the contest for failing to submit his nomination papers on time. The winner of the leadership contest – Diane James – resigned after 18 days, prompting a second UKIP leadership contest that was won by MEP Paul Nuttall on 28th November 2016. He did not survive the 2017 general election and electoral decline and leadership problems have plagued UKIP since 2016. At the same time, the territorial patterning of the Brexit result brought renewed constitutional debate in Northern Ireland and Scotland: parts of the UK which had voted to Remain. Sinn Fein argued that Northern Ireland's Remain vote was grounds to hold a reunification referendum with the Republic of Ireland. The SNP argued that a strong Scottish Remain vote could bring about a second Scottish independence referendum. The Scottish Government published an independence referendum consultation bill (Scottish Government 2016) and set out measures to advance its interests in the EU through its on advisory group on the EU, as well as government and diplomatic lobbying. Along with the governments of Northern Ireland and Wales, it participated in the deliberations on the Brexit process at the Supreme Court in December 2016. That was the immediate political effects of Brexit – without getting into the subsequent snap UK general election of June 2017.

Economically, the FTSE 100 showed some signs of strength after the referendum but other economic indices showed severe stress and signs of economic shock. The FTSE 250 fell markedly on several occasions before recovering later in the year and the Bank of England introduced emergency measures to cope with the crisis.[2] The Bank announced a cut in interest rates to 0.25 per cent on 4th August, holding out the prospect of lower or even negative interests rates (despite years of historic lows). It announced plans to increase the level of quantitative easing funds being pumped into the economy (UK stock markets rose in value as a consequence) and looked to relax the rules around bank capital requirements to encourage lending. The pound sterling fell precipitously on several occasions against the dollar and the Euro – beginning in the early hours of 24th June when early results hinted at a Leave vote. The UK Government began to reexamine its tax and spending plans post-Brexit, with the prospects of serious departures from the long term economic plan advanced at the 2015 election (such as George Osborne's intentions to eliminate the UK's budget deficit and introduce tax cuts for example). Finally, the Scottish Government began to examine measures to stimulate economic growth by advancing infrastructure and job creation programmes to try to prevent the economy from turning to recession. Arguably, the UK continued to face stormy economic times since the June referendum vote as Brexit presented longer term challenges for the economy.

At the 23rd June referendum voters had been invited to determine whether they wanted to Leave or Remain in the EU and the event was only the third time in which a nationwide referendum had been held in the UK. The first referendum was on retaining membership of the European Community in 1975 but it was a long time before the second one on the adoption of the Alternative Vote in May 2011. The third vote on EU membership in 2016 saw a strong turnout of 72.2 per cent. All three of these referendums were held for party political reasons – either to manage internal divisions within the Labour and Conservative parties in government or to facilitate the running of the Conservative-Liberal Democrat coalition government of 2010-2015. However, whilst referendums for many in the UK are a rare experience, there are some areas that have had greater experience of such devices. Wales has had three devolution referendums, Northern Ireland has had two referendums (one sequenced with a referendum in the Irish Republic), whilst Scotland has experienced two devolution referendums plus an independence referendum in 2014. Parts of England have experienced forms of devolved referendum (London and the North East), whilst there have been numerous local referendums on directly elected mayors in England. So, as we shall see, referendum practice is a lot more frequent in recent times, even though the device is not necessarily all that popular with voters and practices are fragmented. Referendums can be popular or unpopular depending on the issue involved and, even in the case of the high turnout Scottish independence referendum of 2014, don't assume that everyone was delighted that it happened. For all the talk of positive public engagement, there were many who wanted the issue to go away and would baulk at any future referendum on the same issue.

Whilst referendums have become a multi-level reality in the UK, we must be careful about linking this reality to broader arguments about direct democracy and the emergence of a consumer democracy (see the arguments by Qvortrup 2007, 2014 and Scammell 2014). For example, the scope of referendums in the UK has been determinedly narrow – almost exclusively about Europe, electoral systems and governance arrangements (even though these can have huge implications for multiple issues and policy areas). Moral or social questions have been decided by parliaments without reference to referendums, nor have major areas of public spending or concern. Taxation, citizenship, same sex marriage, abortion, divorce, nuclear energy etc., have not been subject to referendum. The trigger for referendums is parties and governments not the public – there is no popular initiative for referendums no matter how many change.org petitions appear online. The rules and regulations for the referendums are also determined by governments, in conjunction with the government-funded but independent Electoral Commission.

Since the passage of the Political Parties, Elections and Referendums Act in 2000, referendums in the UK have been regulated by the Electoral Commission. This development brought an end to *ad hoc* rules for the most part, through setting out clearer rules over campaign spending, donations and public information. The Electoral Commission regulates political parties and referendum campaign groups, meaning they may need to register with the Commission if they plan to spend more than £10,000 during the regulated part of the campaign (something like the last 16 weeks). The Commission sets overall spending limits for referendum campaigners in order to prevent a free-for-all, designates lead campaigners and also offers public funding to the two lead campaign organisations: which assumes a simple Yes/No referendum question and campaign. The Commission also has a role in testing referendum questions for intelligibility and accessibility - and on occasion recommending amendments to the question proposed by the government: which was the case with the AV referendum (Electoral Commission 2011a: 42), the Scottish independence referendum and the EU referendum. The Electoral Commission works with government and local government to administer the referendums and is also responsible for public information campaigns to promote both voting and public understanding of the issues at stake in the referendum. What this means is that the Electoral Commission produces information leaflets mailed to each household, has TV and radio adverts and billboards about voting, voter registration and information on the referendum, alongside the campaigners.

In the UK, the public is involved in the referendum campaign and the vote, but in little else. Even though more issues than ever are now determined by referendum in the UK, Switzerland we are not. Finally, consider whether referendums have actually resolved political issues in a conclusive manner? The devolution referendums of 1979 stopped devolution but only for a while: the Scottish Parliament and National Assembly for Wales were established in 1999. The 2014 Scottish independence referendum saw a No vote, but the outcome was enhanced devolution for Scotland and a stronger independence movement than before, determined to have a second chance at a future referendum when circumstances allowed (the significant material change of the Brexit referendum outcome for example, indicated in the SNP's Scottish election manifesto of 2016: Scottish National Party 2016: 24). So, we need to be careful about claiming that referendums are always conclusive, even when they involve binary choices and seemingly clear results.

Understanding Referendum Campaigning

A large part of this study focuses on referendum campaigning and how campaigns operate nationally and especially locally. The local focus is partly about the towns and villages of central Scotland but also about other parts of Scotland too. The study of the campaign will reveal two different faces of referendum campaigning. First, referendums are just like elections and elections in a mature democracy, where parties and voting are well-established. What I mean by this is that parties and governments are heavily involved in referendum campaigning, through party and government leaders, party organisations at the national and local levels, as well as established business and trade union organisations. In short, some of it appears like politics as usual: the same political actors are heavily involved in the campaign and run the show, for better or for worse. They effect the referendum and, in some cases, the referendum certainly effects them: look at what 1979 did to the SNP immediately and to the Conservatives over time and what 2014 did to Scottish Labour. Second, referendums are not politics as usual. The referendum topic can divide political parties from top to bottom, damage their political prospects and have some longer term effects on their functioning. There can be a more fluid politics, in which a referendum can mobilise new political actors and organisations beyond the usual suspects and also drive citizen engagement and interest. Arguably, this occurred in small ways in 1979 and 1997 but in a much more substantial way come 2014 – which saw a high turnout and a range of non-party groups active in the campaign (and paradoxically, a huge increase in some party memberships after the 18th September 2014). Moreover, referendums involve a measure of reflection and campaign learning by participants, with 1979 influencing the Yes campaign of 1997 and, arguably, the 2014 campaign influencing future referendum campaigns in Scotland and the UK more generally ('Project Fear' negative campaigning became a prominent feature of the Stronger

In campaign at the EU referendum in 2016). Some of this is reflected in the interviews, as well in the concluding chapter that looks ahead to future referendums including a possible second Scottish independence referendum.

One development that this book examines across the three referendums is the changing nature of campaigning itself – not least the idea that there are different stages in campaigning, from traditional to professional modern campaigns. Farrell and Webb identified three broad, historical stages in the professionalization of campaigning that will be examined across the three chapters on the referendums of 1979, 1997 and 2014 and in the broader discussion of political campaigning in chapter 3 (Farrell and Webb 1998; Schmitt-Beck and Farrell 2002). In the first stage of campaigning, there was seen to be little campaign preparation, with much of the work done by the party press, with rallies and canvassing, a strong role for the party central offices and volunteers, plus mobilisation of existing supporters through tours by the leaders, posters and leaflets. The second stage of campaigning saw the advent of TV as a mass medium, which saw the development of communication via television and the professionalization of marketing and communications within parties and campaigns. Political messaging became more centralized, with standardized messages and themes – how leaders looked and sounded became important. The third stage involved the use of new technology to professionalise and transform campaigns, with permanent campaign structures and staff, much more direct campaigning and use of targeted messages to sub-groups of the population (Farrell and Webb 1998; Schmitt-Beck and Farrell 2002). Now, the point of these three stages is not to get fixated on their exact timing or development in a sequenced manner. Rather, it is to appreciate that they offer recognizable stages in campaigning and feature many of the practices of modern campaigning and how it has changed. However, as will be argued in the later chapters of this book, aspects of these three stages have blended together to influence recent referendum campaigning – with a strong, local, grassroots level of campaigning that combined traditional campaign practices with modern technology, social media, film and advertising, as well as political carnival: it was both amateur and professional and many of the 'amateurs' were highly professional. There was still space for top-down centralized campaigning, but campaigning was multi-layered and operated nationally and locally too, aided by the new democracy of the internet and social media to create hybrid campaigning. Since the 2014 referendum, the role of social media and its utilization by political parties and referendum campaigns has also advanced considerably though, consideration of that is beyond the scope of this book.

Campaigning Reality

Something worth remembering about political campaigning, both nationally and locally, is that it's a very imperfect activity. The image of political campaigns portrayed on TV may bear little resemblance to actual campaigning, which can be highly disorganized and reactive. The interviews for this book will demonstrate that, but then so do other campaign studies of elections and referendums (see Pike 2015, Oliver 2017, Shipman 2016 and Watson 2015), where lots of things can go wrong even in a winning campaign. Indeed, Ross and McTague's book on the 2017 UK general election illustrated that the campaigns of all the main parties were flawed and led to underperformance (Ross and McTague 2017). For example, there may be no campaign plan or agreed campaign plan or one hastily arranged without sufficient research or organizational preparation. Even where there is a campaign plan, it may not be shared by all of the campaign team – disputes are common place over strategy, tactics, messages, fundraising, etc. Even then, it doesn't mean that people understand the campaign plan and stick to its contents, not in elections or in referendums either: they might just end up reacting to events. So, whilst it's tempting to paint a picture of well-resourced campaign teams of committed professionals, with their detailed opinion polling, focus group testing of messages and materials, with strong design teams for advertising campaigns and online campaigning, reality is rather different from that. Campaigning can be much more chaotic, short-term, uninformed and under-resourced. For every campaign winner, there are losers and this is definitely the case in binary referendums and the loss may not be attributable to the campaign itself. Campaigns are effected by party divisions and interests, staff turnover, lack of resources, buffeting by events and just about everything else you can think of. And, when you are looking at the local level of the campaign, you are dealing with volunteers. And volunteers are just that. They have lives, jobs, relationships etc., to maintain whilst involved in campaigning and have a host of constraints on what they can do. Local campaigns, like national ones, also face challenges from resources, time, organizational capacity and even the weather: ground wars need light and sunshine as opposed to darkness and rain.

The Research for the Book

A lot of the research for this book came about through the work of the Scottish Political Archive (SPA). Since 2010, SPA has collected a range of political material on Scottish politics – individual collections from prominent politicians like Denis Canavan, Jack McConnell and George Robertson, photographs from the *Scots Independent* newspaper, thousands of pamphlets, photos, leaflets and campaign materials from elections in Scotland as well as the devolution referendums of 1979 and 1997 and the independence referendum of 2014. One of the first major projects undertaken by the archive involved research on the devolution referendums – material which was utilized in a number of exhibitions on referendums, in some publications and most obviously here in the pages of this book. The intention was to show both the colour and the content of political campaigning. For example, part of the research centred on an oral history project and involved interviews with national and local campaigners, some by Sarah Bromage as part of Scottish Political Archive project on referendums (all recorded and archived within SPA and referenced in this book with a SPA prefix),[3] with additional interviews by myself to investigate the 2014 experience. It also included local newspaper analysis also by Sarah Bromage, supplemented by myself. The idea was to get a spread of key actors who had been active during the 1979 and 1997 referendums initially and, who could offer perspectives on local campaigning around Stirling University:

meaning in Clackmannanshire, Falkirk and Stirling, hence the focus on local newspapers such as the *Alloa Advertiser, Falkirk Herald* and *Stirling Observer*. In this way, we could make some analysis of the referendums as local campaigning experiences. As you will see, a similar approach has been attempted for the 2014 independence referendum, even though it was a different type of event with a lot more online activism to utilize to understand campaigning. It still featured a mix of local and national campaigning, including some of the same political actors who had been active in 1979 and 1997. And, for this referendum, SPA was able to conduct 'active' collecting on a grand scale, assisted by a large number of volunteers at Stirling University and around Scotland. Of course, what transpired from these interviews are quite different perceptions of the referendum experience. Political activists had different levels of involvement and experience of the campaigns and their own perspectives on what happened and what it meant. There is no single narrative/perception of a campaign, no unitary, unified experience. The interviews offer part of the fragmented picture of a referendum campaign, based on individuals who had both positive and negative experiences. There's also the question of what the campaigners remember from the campaign. Often, from the shape of the interviews, they remembered the things that went wrong during the campaign – the cross-party bitterness and tribal divisions between Labour and the SNP came across loud and clear for example. So, the Yes interviewees expressed lots of (negative) memories from the 1979 devolution referendum but somewhat fewer from 1997. No campaigners were vocal about their campaign problems in 1997. And even then, memory was variable as recall of events can be difficult. Significantly, many of the interviewees and key actors were active across all three referendums, so compared them naturally and with other types of elections too – especially when trying to gauge the level of campaign intensity at the referendum. For supporters of devolution, lessons from 1979 fed into the campaign of 1997. For supporters of independence and the Union in 2014, lessons will presumably feed into a future independence referendum (and some fed into the 2016 EU referendum campaign). In any case, the interviews and material gives us insights into what campaigners felt about the referendum campaigns nationally and on the ground. What the public may have felt is another matter - did they really engage with the campaigns as the campaigners thought? Was it really worthwhile or effective holding public meetings and delivering thousands of leaflets? We do know that public opinion can change at referendums, otherwise Yes would not have grown as a constitutional option from 2011-14. This fact is indicative of the campaign making a difference though, knowing exactly what part of the campaign made the difference is difficult to tell.

Conclusion

Two final points should be made about the book. First, each chapter involves introductory sections that cover the political and economic backgrounds to the referendum itself to give a flavour of the environmental factors at the time such as the state of the economy and the various political/electoral condition of the parties themselves. However, none of these are intended to feature in a deterministic way, they feature as 'shaping' factors around the referendums to help understand the context in which the referendums took place. Every referendum and election has contextual factors that interact with the campaign and the result, through economic and political trends or events, even changes/developments in the campaigns themselves as the campaign can be a dynamic process that involves changes in voter opinion and preferences (Schmitt-Beck and Farrell (2002: 9).

Second, writing about the 2014 referendum and attempting to cover the campaign is fraught with challenges, not least when trying to cover the campaign in one chapter (chapter 6). So, there is no attempt to be comprehensive here and cover all aspects of such a long and intense campaign – that would take several books on the 2014 campaign alone. Rather the chapter tries to place the 2014 experience in political and economic context, examine the national and local campaigning activities and contextualize the result and its aftermath. The referendum has been treated to a range of different accounts from journalists (Cochrane 2014; Geoghegan 2015; MacWhirter, 2013, 2014; Pike 2015, Riddoch 2015, Torrance 2013, 2014), campaigners (Barr 2016; Salmond 2015) as well as academics. Amongst the latter, some have focused on the role of the media broadly speaking (Blain and Hutchison 2016), social media specifically (Quinlan, Shephard and Paterson 2015), whilst some have focused on the wide range of issues that featured in the campaign (Keating 2017; McHarg et al 2016). However, there's a lot more to be written about this particular referendum to add to the existing material.

Endnotes

1. An election that the Conservatives won, in spite of the large increase in electoral support for UKIP to 12.6 per cent.
2. The FTSE was to end the year at its highest ever level of 7142, whilst the FTSE 250 recovered by the close of the year too, to stand at 18,077.
3. These interviews can be accessed here via the University's archive catalogue - http://www.calmview.eu/stirling/CalmView/Default.aspx - searching by the name of the interviewee.

1

The Referendum Experience in Scotland and the UK

Introduction

The United Kingdom is famous for not having a written constitution. Attached to this is the fact that the state has no constitutional provisions for referendums and a history of political hostility to referendums (Bogdanor 1994: 33; Wyn Jones and Scully 2012: 1). Lijphart (1984: 9) even went so far as to state that parliamentary sovereignty in the UK meant that 'because all power is concentrated in the House of Commons acting as the people's representative, there is no room for any element of direct democracy such as the referendum.' Although the UK itself would make exceptions to this aspect of the Westminster model of democracy - and referendums seem to keep cropping up in the UK - these tend to be motivated by partisan considerations, not any deep-seated desire to create a direct democracy. However, take a leap of imagination for a moment and imagine what UK politics would look like if it employed referendums more frequently – more regular referendums on Europe and the Euro perhaps (at least before Brexit arrived), or on divorce, abortion, same sex marriage, nuclear power stations, Trident, capital punishment, income tax rates, HS2 and HS3, Olympic games bids, immigration and citizenship? These may sound far-fetched and yet, these can be topics in referendums in other countries because governments or publics see these as valid referendum questions or because national constitutions require public endorsement at a referendum. Such practices might well make for a livelier form of UK politics if adopted and alter its political practices and behaviour: and impact upon the notion of parliamentary sovereignty.

And yet, despite a negative UK constitutional tradition, referendums have emerged into UK practice in different decades over recent years for a variety of reasons – often driven by political opposition and the need to ensure unity within a political party. They haven't become fully institutionalized as yet, but they aren't the *ad hoc* mechanisms they might have been in the past either (Butler and Ranney 1994: 1). If you are a voter in Scotland and Wales, you may well have lived through three UK-wide referendums and three constitutional referendums on devolution and independence, with more to come in future in all likelihood. In Wales, you will have had the opportunity to vote at the Welsh devolution referendum of 3rd March 2011, then the AV referendum on 5th May that was combined with the election for the National Assembly for Wales: three electoral decisions in just two months. Mostly, the referendum device has been attached to devolution and, since 2001, to directly elected mayors in England. And, from 2000, these referendums were subject to regulation by the Electoral Commission, which set out a series of rules and procedures to govern and facilitate referendums: including public information campaigns on the issues and guidance for participants. So, despite historical hostility and the absence of a constitutional provision for referendums, the UK has developed the practice through legislation, regulation and administration.

However, beyond the UK there are a range of examples of states that utilize the referendum device much more frequently – which is most obviously the case with Switzerland and the United States where referendums can take the form of citizen's initiatives – what Altman defines as citizen-initiative mechanisms for direct democracy (Altman 2014). Indeed, Switzerland has allowed popular initiatives at the national level since 1891, whilst in the USA the first initiatives were adopted as a deliberative device by South Dakota in 1898. However, this broader popular referendum device has not been adopted in the UK despite some fleeting partisan support: Conservatives proposed to allow local referendums in England in 2009 on local issues, if 5 per cent of the local population supported the move (Qvortrup 2013: 3), followed by the capacity for local authorities to be able to hold a referendum to increase the council tax (often linked directly to funding social care). The latter development brought forward a controversial proposal for a local referendum to increase council tax by 15 per cent by Surrey County Council in early 2017, though the proposal was abandoned.[1] Even discussions on the recall of MPs produced a very limited arrangement that made the House of Commons Speaker the trigger point for allowing a local recall vote on a MP under very strict criteria, if 10 per cent of voters agreed. Voters themselves could not trigger this process by collecting signatures, in complete contrast to the manner in which citizen's initiatives operate.[2]

Before 1973, referendums were a largely local matter in the UK – and related to whether local areas would be wet or dry in relation to alcohol: there were 1,131 local referendums held under the Temperance (Scotland) Act 1913 between 1913 and 1965.[3] Similar referendums were allowed in Wales following the Licensing Act 1961, to decide whether alcohol could be sold on Sundays, though it is hard to determine the number of referendums held under this process until the practice was discontinued in 2003. Even when referendums began to be employed in the UK on a wider scale, they were limited in nature. The 1975 EEC referendum stands out as the main exception, as it was the first of only three UK-wide referendums held up to 2016. Slightly more common were devolution-related referendums like the Northern Ireland border poll of 1973 and the Scottish and Welsh devolution referendums of 1979. Even then, referendum use was sparse and these referendums were not intended as precedents.

UK practice only really developed after New Labour's 1997 general election victory, after which referendums became more regular: Scotland and Wales in 1997, London and Northern Ireland in 1998 and then the North East of England in 2004 (which involved questions on both a regional assembly and local government reorganisation). Other devolution referendums in the English regions were proposed – for the North West and Yorkshire and Humber - but never held due to lack of support. Instead, a series of referendums to create directly-elected mayors were held across local authorities in England from 2001 onwards, with 52 local referendums from 2001-2016 which delivered a total of 16 directly elected mayors. And, as democratic experiments, these referendums had their limits. The

64 per cent turnout in Berwick-upon-Tweed in 2001 was impressive compared to the 10 per cent turnout in Sunderland in the same year but turnouts were generally well below 50 per cent and produced No votes for the most part. Turnout for these referendums was higher when combined with another type of election or when using the all-postal voting format and, if successful, the mayor would be elected by a new majoritarian electoral system the Supplementary Vote (Rallings, Thrasher and Cowling 2014: 9). Latterly, the UK experienced a new round of referendums, with a third Welsh devolution referendum in March 2011, the UK-wide Alternative Vote referendum in May 2011, the Scottish independence referendum vote in September 2014 and then the referendum on UK membership of the European Union that was held in June 2016.

Compared to some other countries, the UK's referendum experience is tiny. Take exceptional cases like the United States and Switzerland. In the USA, local and statewide initiatives are commonplace and held on a wide range of matters - particularly in states like California and Oregon – such as on same-sex marriage (for and against), cannabis use, right to privacy, criminal justice provisions, trade union activity, primary election procedures, abortion rights, etc. However, national referendums do not occur. In Switzerland, both the state and the population have the opportunity to call a national referendum. In Butler and Ranney's 1994 volume on referendums, the table that lists Swiss initiatives from 1848 to 1993 runs to 20 pages: beginning with a referendum on weights and measures and ending with one on tobacco product advertising (Kobach 1994: 110-129). A popular initiative can be held if supported by 100,000 voters and proponents have 18 months to collect this level of support. Recent Swiss popular initiatives have included opposition to the construction of minarets in 2009, executive pay in 2013 and two different referendums on immigration in 2014. Overall, almost 200 popular initiatives have been held in Switzerland on subjects as diverse as gambling, health reform, state pension age, accession to the Schengen Agreement, full employment, aviation fuel tax, deporting foreign criminals, tax on spirits, UN membership, etc. And, what is significant about these referendums and referendums in general is that they allow citizens to participate in the debate on a wide range of national, local and policy issues separately from the political parties and candidates for election

4

(Schiller 2011: 10). Arguably there is wider democratic significance here than simply one-off votes on particular topics: especially when the public chooses the topic of the referendum. These initiatives sit alongside wider practice of referendums on an annual basis, every three months at the federal level – but initiatives are common – 12 in 1985 for example, 5 in 1997 and more recently 12 in 2014, 6 in 2015, 7 in 2017 and 10 in 2018.

Understanding Referendums

Constitutional referendums associated with sovereignty are the focus of this book but these are only one aspect of the international referendum experience. Referendums come in multiple forms for multiple reasons and in different types all around the world. Some are held in democracies according to certain rules and patterns, others are held in states or territories that are not democracies or in a state of flux or regime change. Some are states, some want to be states, some are cities, some joined other states or sought to join. The questions, timings and rules all vary, even within individual states. We can at least determine that referendums are popular though. A quick look at the wikipedia entry for referendums in 2014 demonstrated that referendums were held or planned for Bulgaria, Catalonia, Crimea, Denmark, Eastern Ukraine (Donestsk and Luhansk), Egypt, Krakow, Libya, Liechtenstein, Lithuania, Maine, San Marino (2), Scotland, Slovenia, Switzerland (3 sets of referendums in February, May and November), Venice and finally Yemen. And, more referendums would come after 2014 – take the same-sex marriage referendum in Ireland on 22nd March 2015 (there was also a second referendum on the age of the Irish President on the same day) and the snap Greek austerity referendum on 5th July 2015, which saw a 61 per cent No vote on a 62.5 per cent turnout. Or into 2016, the Dutch-Ukraine European Union Association Agreement referendum or the Hungarian migrant referendums and the New Zealand flag referendums. Into 2017, amongst others we saw a second Catalan referendum, plus constitutional reform referendums in Turkey, Puerto Rica and Mali, as well as autonomy referendums in Iraqi Kurdistan, Lombardy and

5

the Veneto. So, we can pretty much guarantee there's a referendum campaign going on some in the world, all year round, every year.

However, while we can count referendums and create an impressive compendium of referendums over time, classifying them is much more difficult as there are various types of referendum. Agreeing on a concrete classification and avoiding overlaps in categories of referendum is more problematic. For example, David Butler and Austin Ranney divided referendums into four main categories (Butler and Ranney 1994: 2-3) – constitutional issues, territorial issues, moral issues and a very unsatisfying category called 'other issues'. Constitutional issues involved dealing with outcomes of revolutions or secessions as well as changes to electoral systems and government structures. However, some of these aspects also leak into the category of territorial referendums. Referendums on moral issues were a much clearer category, with numerous examples of referendums on alcohol, marriage, abortion, same-sex marriage, etc. However, the 'other issues' category is incredibly broad but also understandable as referendums can be held on so many different topics. Take 2014 alone. It may have featured many referendums recognizable as constitutional and territorial but there was scope for much more variety too. The city of Krakow held a referendum on the same day on four different topics – hosting the winter Olympics in 2022, building a metro system, creating a CCTV system in the city and increasing the number of bicycle paths. Meantime, Switzerland held referendums on a national citizen's income, as well as on mass immigration and buying fighter jets for the air force. Liechtenstein held a referendum on public sector pensions reform, Maine was set to hold a referendum to limit bear hunting, whilst Slovenia held a referendum on the personal data of citizens held in the national archives (data on the victims and staff of the Yugoslav security services). In 2016, Italy held a referendum on oil drilling, Queensland on fixed term elections and Hungary on EU migrant quotas.

LeDuc (2003) examined two sets of referendum typologies – on the subject matter of referendums and on the format of the referendums themselves. In terms of subject matter, four broad subject areas were identified: constitutional issues, treaties and international agreements, sovereignty and public policy issues. (LeDuc 2003: 33). Examples of these types of referendums were common before and after the publication of LeDuc's study, with new waves of referendums in Europe associated with the European Union and also developing practices in some post-communist states. Constitutional issues involved changes to constitutions and forms of governance – such as the 5th Republic and Presidential system in France in 1958, 1962 and 2000, Spain's democracy referendums in 1976 and 1978, electoral reform referendums in Italy in 1999 and 2009 and the UK in 2011, regional reform in Italy 2001 and 2006 and Iceland's six-question constitutional referendum of 2012. Referendums on international treaties and agreements were found in Spain over NATO membership in 1986, the large number of referendums on issues associated with European Union membership (Croatia in 2012, France 1992 and 2005, Ireland, Norway and Denmark in 1972, Spain in 2005, Sweden 1994, amongst many others) and joining the Eurozone (Denmark 2000 and Sweden 2003), the EU fiscal compact (Ireland in 2012) and even the Northern Ireland peace agreement of 1998, which had a strong international dimension and required referendums in both Northern Ireland and the Republic of Ireland on the same day (as the peace agreement involved amendments to the Irish constitution). Sovereignty referendums were held in Ukraine in 1991, Quebec in 1980 and 1995 and in Scotland and Wales in 1979 and 1997, though arguably, these could exist as constitutional referendums too. Wales had three devolution referendums from 1979-2014 to establish and then adjust devolution, though Scotland's 2014 independence referendum fitted more clearly into LeDuc's typology where the 'unofficial' Crimean and Eastern Ukraine referendums might also find a home.

Like Butler and Ranney, LeDuc's final category - public policy referendums - is also a very large one that included a wide range of economic, political and social issues. Amongst many examples, it would include divorce (Italy in 1974, Ireland in 1986 and 1995, Malta in 2011), abortion (Ireland in 1983, 1992 and 2002, Italy in 1981), coal power (Slovenia 1999), economic bail-outs (Iceland in 2010 and 2011) nuclear power (Austria 1978, Sweden in 1980, Italy in 1987, Lithuania in 2008 and 2012), medical and tuition fees (Hungary 2008), military conscription (Austria 2013), family code law (Slovenia 2012), spring hunting (Malta 2015), and pensions law (Latvia 1999 and 2008). When you extend the focus to Switzerland

7

and the USA, the number and scope of referendums expands even more, with three referendums in Switzerland on 9th February 2014 on abortion, immigration and railway infrastructure spending, then four more Swiss referendums on 18th May 2014, on defence spending, a national minimum income, restrictions on paedophiles and primary healthcare policy. In the USA, many states allow citizen initiatives, referendums and recall votes, with these votes occurring on a range of policy issues like marijuana use in Colorado and Oregon in 2012, veterans housing in California in 2014 and a cigarette tax in 2016 and opposition to same-sex marriage in Arizona and Florida in 2008. Many state or federal elections – even some primary elections – co-exist with ballot initiatives on a variety of policy issues too so ballot papers can be very crowded affairs in some US states come election day.

Finally, Qvortrup (2005) set out two different typologies of referendums that provide evidence of the diversity of the referendum experience globally. First, Qvortrup (2005: 63) outlined five main categories of referendum, by topic: transfer of sovereignty, constitutional issues, economic issues, moral issues and all other miscellaneous issues that have been put to a referendum. The latter 'type' had the same catch-all appeal as some of Butler and Ranney and LeDuc's categories, but is indicative of the difficulty in finding neat categories for referendums. In any case, it isn't difficult to find global examples of referendums in these different categories as explained above. Though, for the purposes of this book, the categories of sovereignty transfers and constitutional issues are most relevant – with a range of UK examples and a total of 49 independence referendums from 1945 to 2011 (Qvortrup 2014: 25-6), before adding in more recent examples like Catalonia and Scotland. Qvortrup's second referendum typology sought to classify referendum by function not by topic. Here, referendums could be decision-solving, legislative, plebiscitary, legitimating, opposition or tactical in nature (Qvortrup 2005: 104). For Qvortrup, the EEC referendum in the UK in 1975 and the Norwegian EEC referendum in 1972 were tactical and intended to take the issue out of the hands of a divided Labour Party and government and have the choice made by the electorate (Qvortrup 2005: 104): arguably you could make a similar type of argument for the Brexit referendum of June 2016 given divisions within the Conservative Party. Tactical referendums like those on Scottish and Welsh devolution in 1997 were proposed to demonstrate support for devolution and manage the issue against opposition from the Conservatives and House of Lords – hence a second Scottish question on 'tax-varying' powers. Opponents of devolution in the UK in the 1970s also succeeded in forcing referendums onto the Labour government to try to stop the creation of Scottish and Welsh assemblies.

LeDuc (2003: 39) by contrast identified four different forms of referendum: the mandatory constitutional referendum, the abrogative referendum, the citizen-initiated referendum and the consultative referendum. Mandatory constitutional referendums exist in countries like Australia, Denmark and Sweden, where constitutional rules and procedures must be subject to a compulsory, binding referendum. Abrogative referendums have been used in Austria, Denmark and Italy amongst other countries, where the referendum affords a popular veto to citizens over a piece of legislation passed by the national parliament. Citizen-initiated referendums are brought by petition from voters and common in Switzerland and the USA where there are rules on the numbers of petitioners required. Switzerland also features both national and local referendums, where the USA has held local and state referendums (initiatives) on range of different issues from both proponents and opponents of a particular issue. Finally, consultative referendums have been held in Canada, France and the UK. These are initiated by governments and tend to be constitutionally non-binding though some certainly turn out to be politically binding.

For the most part, UK central government has operated as the initiator of referendums at a time of its choosing. However, this is not entirely the case. The Local Government Act 2000 allowed local councils to review their government structures and adopt the mayoral model, but that would need to be accepted through a referendum (there was also a procedure to allow the removal of the directly elected mayor in a locality). The act also involved a process to allow local people to campaign for a directly-elected mayor through collecting signatures on a petition from a minimum of 5 per cent of local voters.[4] The Localism Act of 2011 changed these procedures, so that central government could initiate referendums for directly elected mayors: a curious example of 'localism'. In addition, the Government of Wales Act 2006 empowered the National Assembly of Wales to institute a referendum if 2/3s of elected members supported it: which saw cross-party support in Cardiff trigger the 2011 Welsh devolution referendum. The Northern Ireland Act 1998 contained a provision to hold regular referendums to test opinion on Irish reunification. Schedule 1 of the Act empowers the Secretary of State for Northern Ireland to hold a referendum to determine 'if at any time it appears likely to him that a majority of those voting would express a wish that Northern Ireland should cease to be part of the United Kingdom and form part of a united Ireland.'[5] The provision allowed a simple majority referendum (in contrast to the consensual community consent provisions in the Northern Irish executive and assembly), with a time threshold of 7 years: meaning you could have neverendums, but only at seven year intervals. Finally, according to the legislation, the referendum could be delivered by Orders in Council in the House of Commons, rather than legislation, with the order to include the choice of franchise and the referendum question. The final example of a referendum generated outside central government came in the shape of the Scottish independence referendum of 2014, though this referendum was negotiated with UK central government and took place under the supervision of the Electoral Commission.

Timing, Rules and Franchises

The timing of referendums can be important or, at least, governments and campaigners see them as important. For instance, the Welsh devolution referendum of 1997 was held exactly one week later than the Scottish devolution referendum. Both of these referendums were also held early in the term of the new government when the governing party was popular, as opposed to the experience in 1979. The referendum in the North East of England was intended to be the forerunner of greater English regional devolution. The North East was seen to be the most likely region to vote for devolution, which would then be rolled out across the rest of England. However, instead, the overwhelmingly negative result effectively killed off English regional devolution for a decade and more - although the Conservatives tried to reinvent it with elected mayors and the Northern powerhouse idea between 2014 and 2016 (Department for Transport 2015): with six new directly elected combined authority mayors elected in 2017, without any referendums at all.[6] The Welsh devolution referendum of 2011 was held two months before the election for the National Assembly for Wales to facilitate cross-party unity at the referendum in aid of a Yes vote, knowing that the parties would be competing with each other come the election and any semblance of consensus would have disappeared. The downside was that it meant turnout was lower than if it had been held on the same day as the election. The Scottish government timed its independence referendum to occur by the end of 2014 to allow it as long as possible to reverse public opinion on the independence issue.

In some states, constitutional amendment requires a referendum and the rules around these can be complex (Bogdanor 1994: 28-30). For example, both Denmark and Ireland require referendums to alter their constitutions and there have been several EU-related referendums and, in the Irish case, a range of referendums on moral/ social questions too because of the content of the Irish constitution (the 2015 referendum on same sex marriage was a case in point). In some states, like Switzerland, constitutional amendment requires a supermajority at the federal level, with over 50 per cent of the vote plus support in half of the 26 cantons (LeDuc 2003: 42). In the UK, the corresponding device was the 40 per cent rule from the Scottish and Welsh devolution referendums of 1979: it stipulated that 40 per cent of the registered electorate had to vote Yes for a Scottish Assembly to be created. The rule was added to government legislation as a blocking device by opponents of devolution and has featured in political debates on devolution and constitutional change ever since (Bogdanor 1996). In the Scottish case in 1979, the 40 per cent rule proved a decisive block on devolution as a Yes vote of 51.6 per cent only delivered 32.9 per cent of the registered electorate for Yes, leading to the repeal of the Scotland Act in 1979.[7]

A final aspect of a referendum to consider involves the choice of franchise. In the UK, there were two different franchises for different types of elections: the local franchise for local and devolved elections and the Westminster franchise for UK elections. The first is based on residency and citizenship and includes UK, EU and Commonwealth citizens. The Westminster franchise includes UK citizens at home and abroad, citizens of Cyrprus, Ireland and Malta but not other EU countries, as well as Commonwealth citizens resident in the UK. These rules might sound unimportant, but they have political consequences. For example, Scots residing outside of Scotland but in the UK were unable to vote at the Scottish referendums of 1979, 1997 and 2014, whilst EU citizens resident in Scotland were. Second, the Conservative Government's decision to choose the Westminster franchise for the in-out referendum on the European Union in 2016 effectively disenfranchised the vast bulk of EU citizens from voting on the issue (several million voters at least, who could have tipped the balance of the result). Finally, the Scottish Government successfully instituted the UK's first franchise extension since 1970 by extending the right to vote to 16 and 17 year olds at the Scottish independence referendum in 2014. Furthermore, the Scottish Government then extended the franchise again through legislation in 2015, to enable these young voters to vote at future local and Scottish elections (Scottish Government 2015). So, there is a variant of the local franchise that involves a broader electorate in Scotland alone.

A Role for the People - Citizen's Initiatives

Switzerland and the USA are the most prominent examples of countries that allow the public a role in holding referendums but, whilst they are the most numerous, they are not alone. And, in common with referendums in general, the local measures differ widely in terms of initiation requirements (how many signatures are needed), topics, legislative effects and rules. Switzerland allows federal, cantonal and city referendums, whereas the USA features referendums within individual states alone (including counties and cities), under state laws, with no federal provision or practice of referendums. Constitutional amendments in the USA take place through a complex process involving special majorities in Congress and state legislatures.

Though the scope of local referendums has been broad, some themes repeat themselves over and over again like the citizen's initiatives on marriage/same sex union in many US states in recent years: as the USA experienced waves of ballot initiatives on common themes. The scope has involved local referendums on school language, school districts and alcohol licences in Norway (Schiller 2011: 21); bridge construction, swimming pool construction and waste incineration plants in Finland (Buchi 2011: 216), Nijmegen in the Netherlands held a local referendum on the rebuilding of a historic dungeon tower in the city in 2006 (Qvortrup 2013: 45), whilst in the US, individual states have held referendums on property taxes, immigration, cannabis, budgets, hunting, transportation, pardons, bail bonds, etc. Some states are also frequent users of citizen's initiatives - Arizona, California and Oregon feature prominently here – but the practice is used across a total of 26 states as well as Washington DC on an annual basis (see Reilly 2010 and Reilly and Yonk 2015). Significantly, the USA has seen 2,231 citizen's initiatives since 1904 (Qvortrup 2013: 32): though this number will have undoubtedly risen by the time this book has been published. Finally, the US is significant for having no provisions for federal referendums – and constitutional amendments follow a different and difficult process through elected officials and state institutions as explained above – and a variety of different types of initiatives too.

National popular initiatives have also been used in Hungary, Italy, Latvia, Lithuania, the Netherlands, Slovakia, Slovenia, with eleven EU states allowing popular referendums. Examples have included initiatives on sustainable cattle breeding and hospice provision in the Netherlands, class sizes in Austria and the retirement age in Italy (Qvortrup 2013: 63-5). The rules for holding these referendums were very different – requiring 50,000 signatures in Hungary, 500,000 in Spain and a huge 4,100,000 in France (Qvortrup 2013: 63): meaning it is easy to see why some countries have very few citizen-initiated referendums in practice, as they are difficult to initiate.

The UK Referendum Experience

As discussed above, referendums are varied in format and usage and occur across a range of different countries and parts of countries on a variety of different topics. Making sense of referendum type through classification was also seen to be problematic. However, this reality has not prevented the referendum device from being more common in the UK in recent decades, in spite of a constitutional tradition seen to be hostile to referendums. In the following sections, an outline of some of the main referendums in the UK will be sketched to gain an understanding of both the UK and Scottish referendum experiences, beginning with the first UK-wide referendum on continued membership of the European Community in 1975.

Europe 1975

The first UK-wide referendum was held on 5th June 1975. The referendum itself was post-legislative (Baimbridge 2007: 49), meaning that it was intended to endorse legislation and parliamentary votes from UK accession in 1973 and from UK renegotiation in 1975. The referendum was a consequence of divisions within the Labour Party over EEC membership – a contemporary irony given the last decade of Tory Euro-scepticism - with considerable opposition to joining and then remaining members in the 1970s within the party at all levels. The Labour Government's response to this political reality was to hold a renegotiation on membership, which would be endorsed by a referendum to manage a divided cabinet and party. So partisan considerations rather than great issues of principle were the driving force behind the referendum – a clear parallel with recent motivations in the UK around the EU renegotiation and referendum of 2016. Despite UK efforts to join the European Economic Community (or Common Market) from the 1960s onwards and the final success at accession in 1973, the issue did not appear to be of high political salience for the public at either of the two general elections of 1974 (Butler and Kitzinger 1976: 25). Though, considering the serious economic problems of the time, with eye-watering interest rates, inflation and rising employment, the lack of focus on Europe by voters was understandable.

The European referendum campaign can be viewed as an event in itself though it was one of a series of pro-European campaigns in the 1960s and early 1970s in preparation for UK membership.

For example, between 1971 and 1972, both the Conservative government and party along with the European Movement spent time and resources on public campaigns in support of British membership, with speeches by government Ministers, leaflets, letter-writing campaigns and supportive booklets (Mullen 2007: 73) extending to newspaper and billboard advertising to promote the benefits of being in Europe (Mullen 2007: 74). The 1975 referendum was designed by the UK government in terms of timing, the exact question wording and rules about funding, political broadcasts and government information leaflets. The Yes side of the referendum had government and civil service support and was much better-prepared and organized for the campaign itself – aided by the earlier pro-Europe campaign. On the campaign side, the European Movement had an office, staff and financial resources in advance of the referendum and had already set about creating a volunteer network on the ground, along with a regional organization and distributed 6.5 million pro-Europe leaflets by the second half of 1974 (Butler and Kitzinger 1976: 69). In time, it was overtaken by Britain in Europe, the cross-party organization to run the Yes campaign. Its office opened on 2nd January 1975 and it built up an office of around 140 staff by June, along with 417 local groups, half of which had established local office to campaign and distribute information about the EEC (Butler and Kitzinger 1976: 120). Britain in Europe was determinedly cross-party. Much of its campaigning on the ground was conducted by the Conservatives and Liberals, with little active Labour involvement though, there was Labour Campaign for Britain in Europe, with prominent support from the party and also trade union support for membership. Along with the press, the business community and a range of civic organisations like the churches, there was substantial institutional support for the Yes campaign, which heavily outspent No by £1,481,583 to £133,630, with extensive press advertising (Butler and Kitzinger 1976: 86). The big battalions were on the Yes side and they mobilized to support continued membership.

Local campaigning was a feature of the 1975 EEC referendum, especially on the Yes side. Both the European Movement and Britain in Europe created local groups, often linked to existing political parties, but there were clear patterns to partisan engagement with the referendum. For example, Butler and Kitzinger's post-referendum survey of local campaigning discovered that the 417 Britain in Europe groups had received distinct patterns of partisan support for their activities: 88 per cent reported support from the Conservatives, 76 per cent from the Liberals but only 23 per cent from Labour (Butler and Kitzinger 1976: 120). Labour locally had decided to sit on its hands, reflecting local divisions on the issue and a lack of enthusiasm for Europe at the time: it was not the last time it would do this. The No campaign, through organisations like *Get Britain Out*, claimed to have created 480 local branches outside London and 95 within London come referendum day (Butler and Kitzinger 1976: 135), and despite holding a large number of public meetings, it lacked support and resources for campaigning. It failed to make inroads into the Labour and trade union communities as it had hoped. It had support from both Conservative and Labour figures but its campaigning was poor. However, in all, the level of local campaigning was limited. Only 30 per cent of voters reported any campaign activity in their area, mostly for the Yes side, but even then, this meant that 70 per cent had seen little of the campaign or the issues (Butler and Kitzinger 1976: 158), though widespread newspaper reporting and advertising would have counteracted this information deficit.

The AV Referendum 2011

The referendum on the Alternative Vote was only the second UK-wide referendum and a unique one. It was not the usual 'consultative' referendum. Had there been a Yes vote, the new electoral system rules had to be implemented through legislation. The AV referendum resulted from political compromises between the coalition partners in the UK government: what Liberal Democrat leader Nick Clegg called a 'miserable little compromise'. The only party that favoured AV going into the 2010 UK general election had been Labour – not that it was a strong commitment, more a tactical lure to Liberal Democratic voters and to the party to reach some post-election accommodation. However, it was included in Labour's 2010 election manifesto though during the AV campaign itself, Labour took no formal position. Party leader Ed Miliband favoured AV but many Labour MPs actively opposed the change. The Conservatives were opposed to electoral reform whilst the Liberal Democrats favoured proportional representation, not the enhanced majoritarian system that is AV. However, AV was the maximum change that the coalition was prepared to offer through a referendum held early in the term of the government. In campaign terms, this meant that the Liberal Democrats were the only party campaigning for AV, though damaged by their role in coalition and the unpopularity of their leader Nick Clegg. The No campaign focused on Clegg to exploit his unpopularity and damage AV. With only one party in favour of change, one firmly against and one sitting on its hands, partisan cues to voters were important (Curtice 2013: 220). Two umbrella groups were established to lead the campaign – Yes to Fair Votes and No to AV – with national campaigns and advertising budgets, but little traction on the ground. No concentrated its fire on the unpopular Liberal Democrats (especially to appeal to Labour voters) the costs of introducing AV at a time of austerity and sought to utilize the anti-politics mood in the country (Qvortrup 2012: 112). The Yes campaign sought to explain how fairer votes would improve democracy and make MPs work harder for voters, because they would need to win their seat by a majority. Yes sought to use celebrities in their promotional material rather than politicians but this was not particularly successful, especially given the absence of partisan cues from the main opposition party – Labour.

The result of the AV referendum was clear but unconvincing in terms of public engagement – with No winning by 67.9 per cent to 32.1 per cent. Turnout was 42.2 per cent and the only areas in which turnout was strong was in Scotland (50.7 per cent) and Northern Ireland (55.8 per cent), where the coincidence of devolved elections dragged turnout up. By contrast, the Welsh devolved elections had no such effect, with Welsh turnout at 41.7 percent. The original referendum question was both long and convoluted before testing and reshaping by the Electoral Commission, whilst campaigning participation in the referendum was limited. There were 12 registered campaign groups, with lead campaigners for Yes and No designated simply enough, but engagement by political parties was limited. Whilst the Conservatives and Liberal Democrats registered as campaigners, Labour and the SNP didn't (Electoral Commission 2011a: 99). Spending by two main campaign groups – Yes for Fairer Votes and No to AV – was fairly even, with £2,228,114 for Yes and £2,528,300 for No. However, when other registered No campaigners were added, the final No campaign spend came to £3,472,213: due to spending of £660,785 by the Conservatives and £192,084 by Labour No to AV. The Liberal Democrats were the only party fully supporting a Yes vote but only contributed £62,782 to the campaign.[8] On the ground, campaigning was limited and skewed.[9] Campaign surveys discovered that 80.4 per cent of local Conservative organizations delivered material for the No campaign, whilst 69.6 percent of local Liberal Democrat organizations delivered material for Yes. The corresponding figures for Labour were revealing: only 4.4 per cent of local parties delivered material for Yes, whilst 3.3 per cent delivered material for No: instead the party concentrated on devolved and local elections (Rallings, Thrasher and Borisyuk 2013: 287). Overall, amongst local parties, only 48.6 per cent bothered to deliver AV campaign literature, with most delivered by the Tories for the No campaign and Labour absent from the fray (Rallings, Thrasher and Borisyuk 2013: 287).

The EU Referendum 2016

The third UK-wide referendum – and the second on membership of the European Union – was held on the 23rd June 2016, with the result set to dominate a vast number of political and economic issues for years to come. The referendum was instituted by the UK government which had looked at a variety of different timetables for the referendum – June, September and November 2016 – but chose June as the most helpful timing to achieve a Remain vote (to avoid an expected summer migrant crisis across Europe and Conservative conference in the autumn - see Oliver 2017: 36). The Conservatives had committed to hold the referendum before the end of 2017 and legislation was produced to implement this. Like 1975, the referendum was preceded by an attempt by the UK government to increase the chances of a Remain vote by undertaking a renegotiation of the UK's terms of membership of the European Union on issues related to immigration such as access to a range of benefits, an emergency brake on benefits if immigration was high, the relationship of non-members with the Eurozone and the EU's commitment to ever closer

Union. The idea here was that the Prime Minister would go to the country recommending a Remain vote to keep the UK in a reformed European Union that served the UK's interests better, not least on immigration and sovereignty (how realistic and deliverable these were is another matter entirely, not least because they challenged the EU's principle of freedom of movement). The renegotiation phase began officially when the UK wrote a letter to the European Council on the 10th November 2015. Discussions with the other member states ran for several months and concluded on 19th February 2016. In terms of domestic politics, the renegotiation did not succeed though. Opinion polling found that many voters simply didn't believe the deal would work or went far enough in tackling immigration. Crucially, the deal failed to boost support for Remain (Clarke, Goodwin and Whiteley 2017a: 26) and the late conclusion of the deal meant the effective launch of the referendum campaign without much time to correct that: it didn't create momentum for the Remain side.

In legislative and procedural terms, the referendum was an administrative challenge for the Electoral Commission, government and campaigners due to short time scales. Yet again, the referendum was to be held under one-off rules within the PPERA framework[10] – with the European Union Referendum Act being introduced shortly after the 2015 election on 28th May and becoming law on 17th December. The Act itself required several additional regulations to be instituted - such as the exact date of referendum itself and the timing of the regulated period, the conduct of the referendum and the role of counting officers. There was also an emergency regulation passed on 9th June to reopen online electoral registration because the UK government's electoral registration website crashed before the registration deadline of midnight on 7th June (Electoral Commission 2016: 29-31). Even so, the manner in which the date of the referendum was announced following the UK's negotiations with the EU left little time for the campaign, regulated period and the designation of official campaign groups. It really was a short official campaign of 10 weeks, albeit on an issue that had grown in intensity for years (see Clarke, Goodwin and Whiteley 2017). However, the Electoral Commission did succeed in altering the referendum question from Yes/No to people voting for either remain or leave and ensuring that the referendum was not held on the same day as other elections.

The referendum was not short of campaign groups or public interest as the different groups sought to create local networks of supporters and run local and national campaigns – the Leave groups were particularly effective at creating both an online and local set of supporters for their campaign. One of the Leave campaigns had begun to operate in the immediate aftermath of the 2015 UK election funded by Arron Banks (the Know, which later changed to Leave.EU) – meaning it began campaigning and spending to build its case and a network of campaigners without knowing exactly when the referendum would be held (it could have been held late into 2017). In total, there were 123 registered campaigners with the Electoral Commission, 63 for Remain and 60 for Leave. They spent a total of £32,642,158 and the various groups accepted £30,714,106 in donations as well as loans of £6,071,940 (Electoral Commission 2017: 5). Donations and loans were recorded for the pre-poll period (meaning from 1st February) to improve transparency, whilst spending involved the short regulated period from 15th April to 23rd June (meaning we can only estimate the amount of money spent before this date). The Conservative Party did not register and was officially neutral at the referendum – in recognition of the fact that the party was divided on the issue at all levels from Cabinet downwards (with lots of blue-on-blue political conflict and attacks throughout the campaign). In the meantime, Labour, in spite of a seemingly lacklustre campaign, spent £4,859,243 at the referendum, UKIP spent £1,353,393 and the Liberal Democrats spent £2,223,901 (Electoral Commission 2017: 14). The most surprising spending figure was the £425,622 by the Democratic Unionist Party, some of which was spent outwith Northern Ireland on wrap around newspaper adverts for the Leave campaign. This was one of a range of regulatory issues that the Electoral Commission had to deal with as a consequence of the EU referendum as well as cross-funding of groups, non-registration of groups, donations and loans and non-transparency of spending (Electoral Commission 2017): leading to subsequent investigations by Channel 4 News and the *Guardian* and *Observer* newspapers in 2017 and 2018 involving Vote Leave, Cambridge Analytica and Facebook amongst others.[11]

What did the money go on? Social media, advertising, leaflets, media, rallies and events, public broadcasts, transport, etc. Specific examples of organizational spending give a good idea of where the money went at the campaign - Labour Leave spent £11,867.11 on Facebook, Grassroots Out spent £76,858.80 on media and £46,512.00 on advertising, Leave.EU spent £43,033.72 on rallies and events as well as £119,735.44 on unsolicited material to voters. Vote Leave spent £1,150,740.98 on referendum materials (badges, stalls, posters, balloons, t-shirts, etc.) and £3,289,800.48 on advertising. The Stronger In campaign spent £1,376,842.49 on market research and canvassing (with polling by Andrew Cooper of Populus and voter modeling by Jim Messina) and £2,196,347.71 on unsolicited material to voters (remember the stuff that came through your letter box). In addition to the Stronger In material and the Remain material from political parties, there was also an official UK government information leaflet in support of remaining in the EU – this was not uncontroversial in the campaign due to lack of balance. It cost £9.3 million to have the 14 page leaflet delivered to every UK household and was supported by a government website (Electoral Commission 2016: 103).

Both the Leave and Remain campaigns had to deal with cross-party divisions as they sought to construct effective campaign organisations that could reach different types of voter and party supporter. There were extensive divisions within the Conservatives that indicated a state of civil war over Europe (again) (see Bennett 2016; Shipman 2016), as well as within Labour and UKIP and these effected the types of campaign groups formed as well as the effectiveness of campaigning. For most of the campaign, the Leave side comprised several different groups – Leave.EU, and Vote Leave, as well as the later Grassroots Out (all three applied for lead campaigner designation with the Electoral Commission). On the Remain side, the Stronger In group was the official umbrella group recognized by the Electoral Commission, alongside groups like Labour In and Conservatives In. In addition, there were a host of other registered campaigners across both sides of the issue - there was a Labour Leave group, Trade Unionists Against the European Union, Brexit Express, the Communications Worker's Union, the European Movement, Fishing for Leave, Veterans for Britain, Friends of the Earth, Universities UK, USDAW, Unison, Avaaz Campaigns, etc. (campaigners had to register with the Electoral Commission if they spent over £10,000 and many did, though there were also a range of investigations and complaints about unregulated campaigning: Electoral Commission 2017: 20-24).[12]

The issues in the campaign were broad and complex, but in messaging terms seemed to revolve around immigration (due to the EU's Eastern enlargement in 2004) and the economy, with both sides majoring on themes around these issues. Stronger In's campaign had a strong element of Better Together's 'project fear' from 2014, to try to demonstrate the negative economic and security impacts of Brexit (using experts, economic statistics, gloomy Treasury forecasts, the threat of an emergency budget), whilst the various Leave organisations linked immigration to economic insecurity, employment prospects, lack of funding and capacity for public services (hence painting £350 million a week for the NHS on the side of a bus to show how much the EU cost) and the prospect of future immigration and enlargement (Turkish accession to the EU for example), whilst talking up domestic sovereignty and free trade, with the wrap around slogan of 'Vote Leave and Take Back Control'. So, for the most part, two negative campaigns fought it out over an unloved European Union in a pretty even contest in terms of public opinion as the vote neared. The result of the EU referendum was clear, even though relatively close. Turnout was a relatively high 72.2 per cent and 51.9 per cent voted to Leave, as against 48.1 per cent who voted to Remain. England and Wales voted to Leave, whilst Northern Ireland, Scotland and Gibraltar voted to Remain. The latter territorial pattern of results was just one of the post-referendum challenges to deal with.

North East England

The only referendum for English regional devolution outside London involved the North East of England in 2004. The Labour government had already delivered devolution to Scotland, Wales, London and Northern Ireland through referendums and the English regions faced a range of obstacles to gaining a regional assembly, including a referendum. Initially, Labour proposed to hold referendums in the North East, North West and Yorkshire and Humberside. However, after a series of 'soundings', which indicated how little support there was for regional devolution, Labour curtailed its plan and concentrated on holding a single referendum in the North East. The choice of this area was heavily partisan – meaning, it was a hugely Labour region that was expected to vote to support a regional assembly. For example, Labour had won 28 of the 30 North East seats at the 2001 general election with almost 60 per cent of the vote (Rallings and Thrasher 2006: 929). If voters were to follow Labour's partisan cues, then a Yes vote was likely, however neither party loyalties nor regional identity helped to mobilize a Yes vote (Rallings and Thrasher 2006: 933-4). The North East referendum involved two significant variations on UK referendum experience and, notably, was the first referendum administered under the new Electoral Commission created by the Political Parties, Elections and Referendums Act of 2001. First, despite official criticism of the use of postal voting at UK elections by the Electoral Commission (2004), the referendum was to be all-postal. Second, in some areas, the referendum had a two-question format, asking voters if they wanted a regional assembly and whether they wanted to reorganize their area into a unitary form of local government or not. The referendum featured a passive campaign of leafleting and only 3 per cent doorstep canvassing and 3 per cent telephone canvassing (Knock 2006: 690), with little deep voter engagement in spite of some political stunts and use of celebrities. The all-postal format delivered a turnout of 47.1 per cent, with a huge rejection of an Assembly by 78 per cent to 22 per cent.

Wales 2011

Devolution referendums seem to have become a common feature of Welsh politics, with the 2011 experience following on from the decisive No vote of 1979 and the marginal Yes of 1997. The Welsh referendum of 2011 can be viewed as unnecessary given that there was cross-party support for an issue that was not deemed to represent a 'fundamental constitutional issue' (Wyn Jones and Scully 2012: 3): a relatively minor reform of Welsh devolution rather than something more substantial like taxation powers. Rather the need for a referendum was seen to be all about the need to manage dissent within the Labour Party in Wales (Wyn Jones and Scully 2012: 3). The referendum came about through the procedures established in the Government of Wales Act of 2006, which allowed the Welsh Assembly to propose a referendum with a 2/3s majority of assembly members. Even so, there was considerable maneuvering with the Welsh and UK governments over the provision and timing of a referendum, slightly complicated by the change of UK government in 2010 from a Labour majority to a Conservative-Liberal Democrat coalition administration. The referendum itself was held to allow voters to decide whether the Welsh assembly should gain legislative rather than administrative powers over 20 areas of policy that had already been devolved. This fact explained why the referendum question asked 'Do you want the Assembly now to be able to make laws on all matters in the 20 subject areas it has powers for?' Though there was a clear Yes vote of 63.6 per cent, turnout was low at 35.6 per cent. The referendum experience here was problematic. The issues at stake in the referendum were rather obscure – and a challenge for the parties, campaigners and Electoral Commission to explain - and public engagement was limited, demonstrated by the low turnout. Secondly, Electoral Commission rules in relation to designating lead campaigning organisations at the Welsh referendum effectively failed as True Wales - the No campaign - refused to present itself as a participant as it could not spend the Commission's support grants in the way it wanted: on publicity material rather than on campaign infrastructure (Electoral Commission 2011: 33). This non-designation also weakened the Yes campaign and meant a lack of TV and radio broadcasts and no free mailshot for either campaign: perhaps contributing to the low turnout.

The Scottish Referendum Experience

The oldest form of referendum in Scotland would seem to come in the shape of alcohol prohibition votes held by local councils. These had their origins in the Temperance (Scotland) Act 1913 and allowed local councils to hold a referendum on whether a locality should allow alcohol to be sold (or produced or consumed) until Scottish licensing laws were changed in 1976. Before then, more than a thousand local polls were held, most in the period before 1930 when the prohibitionist movement was strong.[13] Data and information on other types of referendums in Scotland is scant, though the local referendum on Leith's merger with Edinburgh in 1920 came to prominence in 2016.[14] This referendum was not organized by local or national government but by the local newspaper. The merger had been achieved by an act of parliament - the Edinburgh Boundaries Extension and Tramways Act 1920 – but subject to local opposition that the newspaper galvanised.

In more recent times, local authorities have held referendums on a variety of topics. Shetland Islands Council held a referendum in May 1978 in response to the UK government's devolution proposals to establish a Scottish Assembly. The poll saw a 71.8 per cent turnout over the proposal for a special commission for Orkney and Shetland to be inserted into the Scotland bill in parliament. The proposal emanated from the local MP Jo Grimond and received a Yes vote of 89.9 per cent.[15] The former Strathclyde Regional Council held a referendum in opposition to water privatization in 1994. This all-postal referendum opposed water privatization with a No vote of 97 per cent to 3 per cent, on a 70 per cent turnout in Scotland's most populous council area. Edinburgh City council also held a referendum that proposed to introduce a congestion charge to help regulate the city's traffic problems in 2005. Voters rejected the council's proposals by 74.4 per cent to 25.6 per cent on a turnout of 61.7 per cent. In time, the referendum reversal led the council to propose the creation of a tram network for the city – which was substantially late, incomplete and over budget. The third local government referendum held in recent times was Aberdeen City's referendum on two competing proposals to redesign Union Terrace Gardens. Voters supported one project over the other by 52.4 per cent to 47.6 per cent but the whole project was scrapped by the local council in 2012.

The final referendum to discuss here was a private referendum financed by Scottish businessman Brian Soutar, co-owner of Stagecoach – which was notable for being entirely self-funded and one of the few examples of the new lifestyle politics in Scotland.[16] On religious grounds, Soutar opposed the removal of section 28/clause 2A of the Local Government Act of 1988, which had sought to prevent local government and schools from 'promoting homosexuality'. The referendum saw a turnout of 31.8 percent with 86.8 per cent support to retain section 2A as 1,260,846 votes were returned in an all-postal ballot. The result had no direct impact on policy however, as the law was amended anyway, but did offer some lessons to the Scottish political establishment about consultation over social policy changes and relations with religious groups. In retrospect the turnout of the referendum was impressive, though depressed by voters boycotting the referendum itself. This type of initiative was not repeated come proposals to create civil partnerships in 2004 or same-sex marriage in 2014: perhaps reflecting changing public opinion on social issues in the intervening period.

Home rule campaigners over the years also sought to deploy the referendum device to demonstrate support for constitutional change. There were occasional and inconsistent attempts by prominent campaigners to demand government use a referendum in the 1920s and 1930s (Mitchell 1996: 142-44), but the issue failed to develop in contrast to something like the National Covenant petition in 1949. However, there were efforts to hold local referendums on the issue of independence/Home Rule in the post-war period. The Scottish Plebiscite Society, formed in 1946, was active in trying to organize a number of local referendums from the 1950s to 1960. It held a multi-option referendum in the market town of Kirriemuir in Angus in 1949 – with a 85 per cent turnout and 23 per cent support for independence, 69 per cent for a Scottish parliament with similar powers to Northern Ireland and 5 per cent against a Scottish parliament of any kind (Mitchell 1996: 149). A second local referendum was held at the Glasgow Scotstoun by-election in 1950, with a 69 percent turnout and 20,800 ballots in favour of a Scottish parliament with 4,227 against (Mitchell 1996: 152). A third local referendum was held in Peebles in 1959, with a turnout of 75.4 per cent and 66 per cent in favour of a Scottish parliament, compared to 16 per cent in favour of independence and 12 per cent against any Scottish parliament (Mitchell 1996: 155). A further and final local referendum was held in Jedburgh in 1963 by a local political activist, Anthony J C Kerr (Mitchell 1996: 157). It was to be 1993 before another a local referendum on Home Rule was held, under the auspices of the Scottish Constitutional Convention in Falkirk. The referendum was run by local volunteers in conjunction with the Campaign for a Scottish Parliament in December and only 7,788 ballot papers were returned out of 27,828 distributed - a turnout of 28 per cent. (McLean 2005: 148). However, the results saw 88 per cent in favour of a Scottish parliament and 46 per cent in favour of independence (Mitchell 1996: 288).[17]

Conclusion

In the abstract, referendums are simple affairs. With some exceptions, they involve a binary exercise involving a simple Yes/No question that produces a clear answer on a topic. However, beyond that, there is a great deal of complexity about referendums at all levels. Referendums open up significant questions about power and the effectiveness of direct democracy – who can call a referendum, on what subject and when? Who participates in the referendum, who sets the rules etc., are also important questions. In the United Kingdom, the people at the centre of the decisions on referendums are political parties and governments. The public is involved at the campaign and vote stages though public opinion can also act as a driver to influence holding the referendum in the first place. Moreover, the reasons for referendums in the UK are often party-related – Europe and AV – or opposition-generated in the case of devolution. Enhancing democracy is a distant goal in the UK's practices on referendums though it might be a consequence of holding the referendum nonetheless.

Classifying referendums accurately – and in a manner that makes sense to observers – is also problematic as has been argued above. Different authors have used different classifications for referendums because of the diversity of the global referendum experience. In the UK, referendums have been used increasingly but narrowly. The scope of topics has involved types of devolution (the majority of referendums), the EU (twice) and one referendum on electoral reform in 2011. Global referendum practice is much wider than this in terms of topics – especially the range of public policy issues involved – and rules about who can generate referendums through petitions. And, significantly, in some countries like Switzerland and the USA, there is a whole world of distinctive referendum practices with popular initiatives, ballot initiatives and petitions.

Endnotes

1. See https://www.theguardian.com/society/2017/feb/07/surrey-council-abandons-plan-raise-council-tax-15-poll
2. See *Recall of MPs Act 2015*.
3. https://en.wikipedia.org/wiki/Temperance_(Scotland)_Act_1913
4. Local Government Act 2000, clause 34 (4).
5. Northern Ireland Act 1998, Schedule 1, clause 2.
6. The new mayors were created in Cambridgeshire and Peterborough, Greater Manchester, Liverpool City Region, Tees Valley, West Midlands and the West of England.
7. See HMSO (1978), *Scotland Act 1978, chapter 51*.
8. Electoral Commission press release on campaign spending at the AV referendum, 29th November 2011.
9. Trying to archive the AV referendum was near impossible as there was next to no campaign activity by either side in Scotland, with parties concentrated on the Scottish election.
10. The Electoral Commission was keen to have a reformed PPERA with broad rules on referendums in the UK rather than remaking legislation anew for very referendum (Electoral Commission 2016: 10).
11. See https://www.channel4.com/news/data-democracy-and-dirty-tricks-cambridge-analytica-uncovered-investigation-expose and https://www.theguardian.com/news/series/cambridge-analytica-files
12. These included amongst others, *The Sun* newspaper, Vote Leave, the Hungarian embassy, the IMF, Ryanair and JD Wetherspoon.
13. See http://www.scotsman.com/heritage/people-places/the-history-of-scotland-s-dry-temperance-towns-1-4020056
14. Leith was merged despite voting against merger by 26,810 to 4,340. See coverage in *The Herald*, 19th May 2016, p.3.
15. See https://en.wikipedia.org/wiki/Shetland_referendum,_1978
16. http://www.scotsman.com/news/keep-the-clause-the-legacy-1-1388145
17. http://www.falkirkherald.co.uk/news/local-news/falkirk-a-key-independence-referendum-battleground-just-like-in-1993-1-3227516

2

Campaigns, Campaigning and Referendums: Individual, Local and National Campaigning

Introduction

Referendums, especially in the United Kingdom, can involve a distinctive type of politics and political campaigning, albeit one that retains strong involvement from political parties. Pressure groups and civic associations have a role in the referendum campaign but it has been political parties and governments through elections, manifesto commitments, party disputes and coalition agreements, that have determined the existence, timing and rules around referendums: meaning the what, when and where of a referendum. However, despite the centrality of party and government to the referendum experience, the referendum can involve 'abnormal' politics – new issues, new framing of issues, unlikely alliances between political enemies and challenges to party leaders and organizations. In the three cases studied in depth here, these challenges take place during referendums in three different time periods, during which the nature of political campaigning was evolving. One aim of this book is to compare the three different referendums as campaigns, within the context of changing campaign practices and environments. In a very general sense, political campaigning in the UK has moved from traditional formats to levels of professionalization associated with political marketing, new technology and direct campaigning practices associated with the development of a 'consumer democracy' (Scammell 2014), characterized by modern political marketing: often loosely referred to as the Americanization of British politics. However, as we shall see, traditional forms of campaigning remain popular and widespread and, arguably, experienced something of a resurgence in 2014. The book will argue that the Scottish referendum experience in 2014 involved a blended campaign experience in which old school traditional campaigning met up with new technology and extensive social media usage, which was practiced in both centralized and decentralized manners by a range of organizations and individuals. Some of this was campaigning as usual, in either the traditional or modern sense but some of it also resembled political carnival, with a wider range of campaigning repertoires and activities than we would normally see in an election campaign.

Understanding Political Campaigns

One striking thing about the environment of the three different referendums are the very different types of campaign conducted due to changing campaign techniques, technology and the media. Political campaigning has changed substantially over the last 50 years to become more professionalized and influenced by political marketing and communications specialists. However, one of the striking things about the three referendums and especially the 2014 experience was that traditional campaign techniques remained strong and actually deeply embedded in campaign repertoires in spite of technological advances. For example, 2014 was probably the first real social media political campaign in the UK, conducted through Facebook, twitter, instagram and a range of other channels with these mediums used to organize and orchestrate the campaign, build grassroots networks and also popularize campaign messages and events through the design and deployment of infographics. Significantly, these multi-media practices were not merely the domain of centralized campaign organisations, but widely used by a range of smaller organisations as well as local campaign groups and individuals (simultaneously facilitating centralized and decentralized campaigning). However, aspects of the campaign in 2014 would be recognizable to anyone active in any election campaign in the UK in the twentieth and twenty-first century: leaflets, posters, stalls, doorstep canvassing, public meetings, badges, etc. All the traditional campaign techniques were on show. In addition, the range of actors in the referendum campaign expanded compared to normal elections as well as to the previous referendums. New actors and organizations were established and these utilized a combination of traditional and post-modern campaign techniques to promote their positions, demonstrating a DIY dimension to campaigning by skilled activists and 'creatives', independent of the main campaign organizations and political parties. This development did not always fit neatly with the more centralized campaign messages of the main campaign groups.

For several decades, academics have been trying to capture developments in political campaigning and the transition from traditional to modern campaign techniques as political parties became more professional in their campaign activities. Charting this transition has not been an exact science as parties have not adopted the same methods at the same time and any attempt to accurately periodise the adoption of campaign techniques is difficult. There were also significant differences in campaigning across different countries, despite the evident 'Americanization' of campaigning: the use of direct mail, candidate-centred campaigns, databanks and micro-targetting, etc. However, the overall picture of change is a convincing one and, these changes overlap with the three referendums in this book, which utilized a range of campaign techniques that demonstrated the modern or post-modern campaign in action. Overall, it is useful to maintain a degree of skepticism about the growth and effectiveness of modern or post-modern campaigning. Often, modern campaigning simply involves adapting traditional campaign techniques rather than replacing them (Scammell 1995: 6). For example, political marketing using direct mail to target distinct segments of voters relies on doorstep or phone canvassing to collect simple voter data, processed through new technology. Parties may use socio-demographic software like Mosaic, Experian or Google Analytics to identify key target groups,[1] but often volunteers and old-fashioned shoe-leather are central to the success of this venture. Without the local workforce in the constituency – usually volunteers

– any professional, national campaign would struggle when it came to targeting its efforts effectively (Johnston and Pattie 2014: 17) though more recent online developments have facilitated more effective targeting through online research (Fisher 2015): and none more effective than the Conservatives at the 2015 UK general election, which delivered an unlikely majority (Cooper 2016, Ross 2016). This campaign operated under the radar and involved two and half years of data collection and research to understand key voter segments, design campaign materials and relentlessly target groups of voters in key constituencies though multiple, tailored mailshots and emails (Cowley and Kavanagh 2016: 59, 63, 261). Though both Yes and Better Together made extensive use of social media at the 2014 referendum, the costs involved were low. For example, in the 2014 regulated period from 30th May to 18th September, Yes Scotland spent only £1,094.94 on Facebook advertising, whilst Better Together spent £2,888.88 on adverts and purchasing likes on Facebook (Electoral Commission spending returns 2014).[2] These figures were dwarfed by the subsequent referendum spending by such as *Britain Stronger In* at the EU referendum of 2016, which spent £812,478.34 on Facebook advertising during the regulated period or the reputed £1.2 million spent by the Conservatives at the 2015 UK general election (see Moore 2016). Since then, all parties have developed their social media campaign activities and spending along with accusations about the production of 'dark' advertising and covert funding of campaigns.[3] Targeted social media campaigning has come on in leaps and bounds since the 2014 referendum. However, during that campaign, extensive volunteer networks, friends, family and political organisations were active in sharing referendum campaign material widely through social media so organic reach was successful: getting volunteers to promote the message for free was one way of avoiding the large advertising costs for social media and because so many people were doing it that it reached wider audiences rather than just existing supporters.

Writing back in 1997, Pippa Norris sought to outline three broad phases of election campaigning by political parties in the UK: a pre-modern phase that ran from the 19th century to the 1950s; a modern phase from the early 1960s to 1980s, during which TV became a vital campaign medium (1959 was seen as the first TV election in British politics), as campaign techniques came to be imported from the United States; and a post-modern phase from the early 1990s on, in which parties deployed permanent campaigning, professional marketing activities and local campaign activity became centrally-controlled (Norris 1997), but gave new life to local campaigning as marginal and target seats and constituency campaigning took on renewed importance (Johnston and Pattie 2014: 17). The operationalization of these three time periods into a detailed table of phases and practices was attempted by Plasser (2002), with discussion of the role of the media, campaign coordination, dominant campaign paradigms and the levels of campaign preparation (Scammell 2014: 19). These time periods may be broad and slightly overlapping across elections and parties, but they are recognizable. Denver and Hands' studies of local campaigning, which will be referred to below, sought to divide campaign times into Fordist campaigns, that focused on broadcasting to mass electorates, with post-Fordist campaigns, that used marketing techniques to target sections of the electorate, using surveys of campaigners to examine developments in campaign techniques and technology (Denver and Hands 2006). Denver and Hands also sought to operationalize and test the notions of campaign modernization on the ground, through the functioning of central and local party organizations during the campaign. Subsequent authors sought to test these aspects of campaigning more fully, in addition to focusing on the impact of local campaign spending, the role of party members as well as volunteers (Fisher, Fieldhouse and Cutts 2014): as local campaigning was seen to have become increasingly important as opposed to just national campaigns.

As discussed earlier in chapter 1, Farrell and Webb (2002) (elaborated in Schmitt-Beck and Farrell 2002: 10-11) took a slightly different approach and sought to divide party campaigning into three different stages according to changes in technology, resources and thematic developments, to try to explore all the different campaign developments in sequence:

Stage 1 – little campaign preparation, reliance on traditional communication through the party press, rallies, canvassing and local campaigning, targeted on traditional supporters through campaign events and propaganda (Farrell and Webb 2002: 4-5).

33

Stage 2 – campaigning became more professionalized through the medium of TV, longer term campaign planning, use of marketing by central party bureaucracy and employment of campaign professionals and national campaign strategies and messages, concentration of campaign resources at the centre, with a focus on party leaders and the media (Farrell and Webb 2002: 5).

Stage 3 – the arrival of new technology and along with it, the permanent campaign, direct marketing and campaigning through direct mail, email, etc., campaigning professionals take over from party organisers, with the campaign focused on consumers rather than supporters to target particular groups during the long campaign (Farrell and Webb 2002: 6).

Whether stage 3 remains viable as a category these days is a good question given that post-modern campaigning now involves extensive use of social media by parties, campaign groups and individuals. As technology has evolved in terms of both centralization and decentralization since Farrell and Webb's study, there is a case for thinking about a modified stage 3 or a new stage 4: though given the blended nature of campaigning, that combines traditional, modern and post-modern campaign techniques, a new category might not be so important to distinguish. In this category, social media is used as a promotional marketing tool, a networking organizational tool but also an attempt to micro-target segments of voters through collecting data on voters via cookies when they connect to websites or through online surveys (this latter aspect would favour central party direction and control). Meanwhile, online platforms like Nationbuilder are used to coordinate and publicise campaigning and act as a central organising hub for parties and referendum campaign groups.

Besides broad studies by Norris and Farrell and Webb, which were intended as comparative contributions across a range of advanced industrial democracies, UK scholars have sought to examine campaign professionalization in detail in recent years, particularly through intensive study of the 2010 UK general election. Scholars like Fisher and Denver (2008) sought to adopt Farrell and Webb's staged approach at the local level of campaigning to focus on individual constituencies in the UK. They used these stages to develop and test three different campaigning indexes: an index of traditional campaigning, an index of modernization and an index of centralization. The traditional index featured campaign practices such as leafleting, posters, doorstep canvassing and public meetings (Fisher and Denver 2008: 804). Modernization involved the use of computers, election software, telephone canvassing and direct mail (Fisher and Denver 2008: 823). The index of centralization involved the extent of national/regional control of campaigning, the use of centralized databases and canvassing and the level of central direction/control of local activities (Fisher and Denver 2008: 823). Testing party campaigning with these indexes found a decline in traditional campaigning from 1992-2005, though traditional campaigning remained important (and saw a slight revival in 2005). In addition, a good deal of the local campaign was now centrally-driven or delivered through phone banks and direct mail, through national call centres that focused on target seats at election time (Fisher and Denver 2008: 810). Finally, campaign professionalization was not limited to central party bureaucracies, as parties had sought to professionalize local parties and volunteers through training programmes, use of local agents, regional coordinators, etc., to improve campaign coordination, targeting and local skills bases (Fisher and Denver 2008: 812). Subsequent campaign studies sought to build on these dimensions to create a campaign intensity index and one that included e-campaigning (Fisher, Cutts and Fieldhouse 2011: 820). Bale and Webb (2015) for example, started to ask party activists whether they shared Facebook postings by their parties and/or tweeted/retweeted their messages.

The Rise of Professional Campaigning

The professionalization of campaigning was associated with the post-1979 efforts of Mrs Thatcher's Conservatives and then Labour under Neil Kinnock and Tony Blair. Each party sought to utilize modern marketing ideas and practices, in-depth voter research and the mass media to appeal to voters: with practices imported from the USA. Messages, symbols, conference sets, party colours and individual politicians were all up for rebranding and restyling, whilst party messaging become more important and controlled by media managers within the campaign (see amongst others Franklin 2004, Lees-Marshment 2014). The rise of spin doctors was part of this process. Opinion polling and testing of messages and positions became extensive and focus groups were used to test policies and idea (see Gould 1998). Having said that, some aspects of modern campaigning were in evidence before this. Indeed, it's worth remembering that the first TV election in the UK was actually in 1959 – 51 years before the UK adopted Presidential-style TV debates between the party leaders of the Conservatives, Labour and Liberal Democrats at the 2010 UK general election. Such professionalization was accompanied by more professionalised and centralized political parties at the centre, but also the hollowing out of parties on the ground, less of a role for party members and a reduction in party memberships in the UK. Some of the campaign professionalization appeared modern or post-modern but it is worth remembering, that part of its function is to compensate for the decline in party memberships and local campaigning. As local, face-to-face campaigning is seen to be most effective in engaging voters and mobilizing support, there are limits to the benefits gained from impersonal centralized campaigning and political marketing (Johnston and Pattie 2014: 152): yet parties were often left with little else due to lack of activists on the ground – something which has clearly changed in recent years as some political parties increased membership dramatically in recent years.

The period of campaign professionalization also saw the development of what Pippa Norris referred to as 'hypermedia campaigning' (2000: 178): that politics had become multichannel due to the growth of 24 hour news and publishing, as well as long-term and relatively permanent. And, this depiction occurred before the explosion in social media campaigning with Facebook, twitter and the blogosphere. However, according to Norris, the new multichannel environment created opportunities for political parties and campaign groups to utilize pre-modern, modern and post-modern campaign tools rather than rely on one particular technique or channel: making for more complex campaign opportunities and challenges at elections and referendums. This development was particularly evident in the 2014 independence referendum, at which a variety of campaign types were deployed by a wide range of actors, some from parties some distinctly non-party: arguably, it created a hypermedia campaign environment.

The Return of Local Campaigning

In the last 20 years, several studies began to examine the importance of local campaigning at British elections (Denver and Hands 1997; Johnston and Pattie 2014). Rather than accept that elections were purely influenced by national factors and centralised campaigns or sociological factors, these studies began to examine the local campaign effects on elections. These effects were particularly important because of the nature of the UK's first past the post electoral system – namely that it created a relatively small number of marginal seats which saw intensive election campaigning, as against a much larger number of safe seats where election campaigning was much less in evidence and sometimes non-existent. Targeted campaigns in key seats vital to electoral victory were one reason for a renewed emphasis on the local campaign – as parties expended resources identifying support in marginal constituencies and ensuring it turned out to vote on election days (Johnston, Cutts, Pattie and Fisher 2012) - as were electoral dealignment and new technology, which allowed local and central party campaigners to make local campaigning more efficient and effective (Denver, Hands and MacAllister 2004: 290). Establishing that local campaign activism was growing was one thing, but determining its effect was another: did it actually effect local elections results and contribute to a national electoral picture? Studies by Pattie and Johnston sought to use local campaign spending by the Conservatives, Labour and Liberal Democrats to provide one measure of campaign intensity at the local level, especially in marginal seats (Pattie and Johnston 2009, 2014). Denver and Hands (1997, 2006) used post-election surveys of local organizers to measure the content and intensity of the campaign and develop an index of post-Fordist campaigning, whilst party membership surveys were used to determine local involvement in campaign activities (see Whiteley and Seyd's 2003 study of Labour and Liberal Democrat constituency campaigning). Significantly, it's not just that local parties are involved in intense campaigning, but also that many are responsible for raising and spending substantial amounts of money at and between elections. For example, aside from national campaign spending of £31.5 million, local parties and individuals were responsible for spending £25.2 million on behalf of 4150 candidates at the 2010 UK general election between 1st January and 6th May (Johnston and Pattie 2014: 28). At the 2015 UK general election, the spending pattern was slightly different with £37.3 million spend by the political parties and £22.6 million by local parties and candidates. The balance may have shifted but the amount of local spending remains substantial (Electoral Commission 2016: 19) and the lines between national and local spending has become blurred as revealed by the Channel 4 investigation into Conservative election spending in 2015 involving the party's battle bus, staff and hotel costs.[4]

The level of political activism by party members has also been examined, with studies of the Conservatives (Whiteley, Seyd and Richardson 1994), Labour (Seyd and Whiteley 1992), Liberal Democrats (Whiteley, Seyd and Billinghurst 2006), Scottish Greens (Bennie 2004) and more recently the Scottish National Party (Mitchell, Bennie and Johns 2012).[5] The latter study found almost a third of SNP members were very/fairly active in campaign and party activities, with 21 per cent of members spending 1-2 hours a month, 15.5 per cent spending 2-10 hours a month and 6.4 per cent spending 10 hours or more a month (Mitchell, Bennie and Johns 2012: 87).[6] Such levels would increase during election time, though some local parties had regular election-type activities for members across all the parties to develop/maintain support and make progress in marginal constituencies. Of course, it's not just party members who are active in local campaigns come election time. In addition, there is a range of party supporters who join in with campaigning, whilst not actually joining the party – a loose form of association more familiar in the US party system. Given the shrinkage of many, though by no means all, political parties in the UK and the general inactivity of most party members, the role of non-members as part of the electoral workforce was vital. Such supporters were involved in activities like leafleting and polling day work rather than canvassing (Fisher, Fieldhouse and Cutts 2014). The role of non-party volunteers at this level was an interesting development of relevance to the referendum experience, especially with the potential role for Yes and No supporters outside the political parties to boost the ground campaigns of the different referendum campaigns (Adamson and Lynch 2014: 155).

Referendum Campaigning

Referendum campaigns have their own dynamics according to the issue involved, the various political actors and the economic and political context of the campaign. Even referendum time periods can prove influential. The 1979 devolution referendum was brief and conducted in challenging weather conditions and adverse economic circumstances. The 1997 campaign was slightly longer, planned by the Yes side in advance and influenced by the landslide Labour victory of the UK general election and the 18 years of Conservative rule that preceded it. The 2014 experience was very different. It was the longest election campaign in UK history, beginning officially in May 2012 and lasting until September 2014. The long campaign was certainly a challenge to referendum campaigners – how to sequence campaigning, spending, messaging, etc., over such a long time period. It was also a challenge to political activists more used to the short campaign cycle of intensive campaigning in the last 5 weeks or so of a general election. The type of campaigning that takes place at referendums is also variable. As discussed briefly in chapter 2, some UK referendums saw extensive local and national campaigning, like the 1975 EEC referendum, whilst others like the AV referendum saw limited local campaigning apart from the Conservatives on the ground, but a centrally-driven media campaign at the national level.

Regardless of their length, referendum campaigns can produce their own dynamics as they are dynamic events in which various developments, factors and campaign issues can shape the outcome – some planned by campaigners, parties and governments, some unplanned. This point is shorthand for opinion changing over the course of a referendum campaign as voters digest the issues and respond to the campaign and to events (LeDuc 2002: 152-3). Measurements of campaign volatility have shown significant shifts

39

in opinion across referendums (LeDuc 2007: 29) and we will find such volatility across all of our examples (though it only changed the result in one case in 1979, technically on the 40 per cent rule). Campaigns can also help crystalize or solidify opinion rather than change it (Vreese 2007: 15). Each referendum topic and campaign involves a series of challenges. How do voters respond to the issues, or to party campaigning? Do voters follow party cues on a referendum topic or is the party divided on the issue and offers uncertain cues to voters? Is the government or political leaders popular or unpopular? (creating second order campaign effects – see LeDuc 2002: 146). Does the campaign put something else on the ballot paper or redefine the question – as Trudeau did with 'renewed federalism' at the 1980 Quebec referendum (LeDuc 2002: 156) and The Vow did at the 2014 independence referendum by offering devolution reform with a No vote? Are voters shaped by events like televised debates or campaign events or the evolving campaign discourse that seeks to frame the referendum topic in a particular way (Vreese 2007: 1-2)? Finally, are voters risk averse? Is it easier for status quo campaigns to win referendums by focusing on the problems with change through a negative campaign that sees a reversion to the status quo during the campaign as referendum day nears (LeDuc 2007: 34)?

Political parties have been central to the referendum experience in the UK and are important in other countries too. Almost exclusively, it has been political parties who have proposed and instituted referendums, and they have been major campaign actors in the referendums too, as part of the Yes and No campaigns. Despite the decline in importance of political parties – as memberships have fallen (until dramatic increases in recent years), voters have experienced partisan dealignment and electoral turnouts have slipped – they remain key political institutions in democratic politics and to referendums in the UK, shaping the issues, deploying government resources and political discourse (Adamson and Lynch 2014: 3). When they are inactive – like Labour at the North East regional assembly referendum of 2004, they can effect the result. In other countries, pressure groups and civic organisations play a role in instigating referendums and acting as campaigners. There was definitely some of this dimension in Scotland, especially in 2014 as we shall see, but parties were crucial in providing government, campaign staffing, expertise and resources, networks of members and elected officials, local organization on the ground as well as strong media profile and communications capacity with key leaders able to communicate political messages around the referendum. Even where umbrella referendum campaigns are created – Scotland Says Yes, Scotland Forward or Better Together – they are comprised of political parties, which had a central role in their direction and the parties 'lent' their staff and expertise to the campaigns.

Finally, parties matter as they are often primary carriers of the message at a referendum and voters look for cues from their political parties to understand the issue and how they should vote (see Pattie, Denver, Mitchell and Bochel 1999; Liñera and Cetra 2015; Clarke, Goodwin and Whiteley 2017). The party cue can be clear – Labour says vote X, the SNP says vote Y, or it can be muddled and disrupted. For example, at the 1979 devolution referendum, Labour Vote No was intended to disrupt the official party's cues on devolution. It was helped by the fact that devolution was a controversial issue within Labour and it had high profile supporters who were prepared to campaign against the government's official position in the media and on the ground - which will be apparent in the discussion on Tam Dalyell later in this chapter and on the 1979 and 1997 referendums in chapters 4 and 5. Notably, Labour divisions over devolution did not re-emerge publicly come the second devolution referendum in 1997 due to careful party management plus timing. Finally, some disruption in party cues was evident at the 2014 referendum as some Labour (with Labour for Independence) and Liberal Democrat voters disobeyed their parties to vote Yes.

The Umbrella Campaign Groups

Referendums offer particular challenges for the nature of campaigning, not least in the UK, where designation rules created by the Electoral Commission require there to be official umbrella campaigns for each side at a minimum. And, such official status would involve public resources, spending limits and legal obligations during the campaign. Whilst many referendums involve dedicated lead campaigners, these are far from the only participants. Parties, civic groups, businesses and individuals can register as campaigners and participate in referendums – but these vary widely from referendum to referendum. Umbrella groups face a number of challenges at a referendum. Are they seen as legitimate? Can they generate resources and implement effective campaign strategies and, importantly, can they manage the internal tensions of their component parts. Often, umbrella groups at UK referendums are effectively comprised of representatives of the political parties (sometimes with a non-party figurehead) and cross-party conflict is a feature of the internal and external lives of the campaign: as the campaign may involve very unlikely bedfellows with their own political agendas. For example, party divisions bedeviled the Yes campaign of 1979. So much so that there was no effective umbrella campaign for Yes, but a series of campaign groups and parties seeking to mobilise support for a Scottish Assembly in a fragmented manner. Nationally and locally, there were divisions between Yes campaigners and the political parties at all levels. As we shall see in chapter 4, the Yes campaign of 1997 was explicitly constructed to avoid a repeat of such divisions, as they were interpreted to have contributed to the failure of devolution in 1979. Similarly, participation in an umbrella campaign group can have political consequences beyond the referendum itself. The Better Together umbrella group at the independence referendum was largely Labour-led and implemented a successful campaign strategy to deliver a No vote. However, internal disputes were legion (Cochrane 2015, Pike 2015) and Labour suffered immense electoral damage following its participation in the campaign even though it had tried to create its own No campaign in 2014 in the shape of United with Labour in order to protect itself from over-identification with its Better Together partners (Shaw 2014). Unfortunately for Labour, winning the referendum came to mean losing just about everything else in Scotland at the May 2015 general election. Worse was to come with the Scottish elections of 2016, at which it lost more FPTP seats and trailed in third behind the SNP and the Conservatives in terms of MSPs.[7]

Civic Groups and Campaigning

One of the defining features of the quest for self-government in Scotland is that it has enjoyed a long-lasting and diverse national movement (Mitchell 1996). This movement has pursued devolution, Home Rule and independence and employed a range of electoral and non-electoral strategies to advance its goals. The Scottish National Party may have become the most prominent component of the movement, though this was not always the case. Over time, various organizations like the Scottish Home Rule Association, Scottish Convention, Scottish Plebiscite Society, Campaign for a Scottish Assembly, Democracy for Scotland, Scotland United and a host of others have been active in promoting the case for Home Rule (McLean 2005). Sometimes their focus was on influencing political parties. At other times, they sought to influence public opinion and create grassroots organizations. Often, their efforts focused on promoting the Home Rule case between elections, often when a pro-change outcome had not been forthcoming. This was very much the case with the Destiny marchers after the 1992 UK general election saw the re-election of the Conservatives, with a series of walks across Scotland to publicise the case for Home Rule followed by Democracy for Scotland establishing and maintaining a permanent vigil outside of the proposed site for the Scottish assembly at the foot of Calton Hill in Edinburgh from 1992-97. Groups such as these had a role at the 1997 devolution referendum but a much more substantial one at the 2014 referendum. At this referendum, political parties and the two official campaign groups Yes Scotland and Better Together shared the stage with a very broad range of organizations, most from the national movement rather than the pro-Union side as a broad Yes movement developed during the referendum. Some of the organizations were sectoral groups formed by Yes Scotland like Academics for Yes, Fishing for Yes, Sport for Yes, so linked to the official Yes organization, but many were autonomous and indicative of the formation of new social movements around the national question: such as National Collective, the Radical Independence Campaign and Women for Independence: Independence for Women. Better Together also created some sectoral groups like Academics Together and Women Together, though had less impact on new group

43

formation. Arguably, the range of individual organizations made Yes much bigger, with a range of autonomous groups campaigning in very different ways – much of which would be unrecognizable as election campaigning. Much of it was organized through social media and volunteer networks. It tended to be crowd-funded and part of a 'thousand flowers blooming' approach by different parts of Yes, rather than something centrally-controlled and managed. It spawned National Collective, Radical Independence, Women for independence, Business for Scotland and Labour for Independence amongst others. Major events like the independence march and rally in 2012 and 2013, were created by local activists not Yes Scotland. The Yestival tour of Scotland was created by National Collective. Local campaigners raised funds to establish Yes shops, Yes buses and vans and advertising trailers. Films, websites and blog sites were also funded through public support via online crowdfunding platforms (usually indiegogo). There was diversity of engagement beyond the political parties.

Whilst the amount of non-party campaigning in 2014 was much larger than anything that went before in Scotland's referendum experience, there were other examples. For example, the Bus Party offered a non-partisan platform for members of the artistic community to discuss constitutional change in 1997 and 2014. The Bus Party – so-called because it travelled the country on a bus – was created by the Home Rule pressure group Common Cause and influenced by citizen's initiatives in West Germany orchestrated by Günter Grass in the mid-1960s (Ascherson 2003: 126). Common Cause sought to use their local contacts to create a series of events for the Bus Party, which toured Scotland in a small blue bus in the week before 11th September, with talks, music and discussion from Willie Storrar, William McIlvanney, Neil Ascherson and others. The intention was to take the Home Rule issue away from politicians and parties and out into communities in a more imaginative approach to campaigning and citizen engagement than traditional campaigning allowed. Some of this group reassembled as the Bus Party 2014, with a tour of 16 venues in May christened the Listening Lugs tour (lugs are a word for ears in the Scots language). This Bus Party was slightly more politically ambiguous, comprised of independence supporters but also Home Rulers too. The tour went from Wick to Wigton,

Dalmuir to Falkirk and Lochgelly to Stromness. The group held readings of poetry, short stories, played music and asked the public to write their wishes for Scotland on a huge scroll. Storrar, Ascherson and Billy Kay were back, along with James Robertson, Janet Paisley, David Greig, Karine Polwart, Ricky Ross, Janice Galloway, etc.

Old Campaigning, New Campaigning: Tam Dalyell and Jim Sillars

One way to understand the changing nature of campaigning across the different Scottish referendums is to focus on the activities of some prominent individuals who played a role in the campaigns. Though there were 35 years between the 1979 and 2014 referendums, some people campaigned at both of them and at the referendum in 1997 too. Some were or became prominent politicians; others were party members or individuals. As we shall see in subsequent chapters, each referendum saw different campaign styles and took advantage of developments in campaign professionalization but also adopted traditional techniques too. Both of the individuals here were proponents of traditional campaigning, through use of the traditional media and extensive face to face campaigning in 1979, but this extended into the use of social media come the 2014 campaign. Tam Dalyell was MP for West Lothian (then Linlithgow) from 1962 to 2005. He was a prominent critic of devolution in the 1970s and helped lead the No campaign at the referendum through acting as Vice-Chair of Labour Vote No: which helped to neutralize Labour support for devolution and galvanise opposition amongst the party's electorate. Some of Dalyell's political focus was on the progress of devolution legislation through the House of Commons, where he was active in debates on the issue along with George Cunningham and Enoch Powell – hence the idea of the West Lothian question, which was named after Dalyell's constituency. However, Dalyell was also a hyperactive campaigner at the referendum itself through extensive letter-writing to local newspapers across Scotland as well as speaking tours to a variety of audiences both on his own and in tandem with Jim Sillars of Scotland Says Yes. What Dalyell engaged in was old-style campaigning – very different to current campaigning – reliant upon his speaking talents, his pen as well as attention to local newspaper treatment of the devolution issue. Though Dalyell published his autobiography in 2011, it barely mentioned the devolution campaign or his role in the referendum - indeed, he spent more time in the book relating his role in an Inter-Parliamentary Union visit to Brazil in 1975 than on devolution (Dalyell 2011). However, examination of local newspaper coverage of the 1979 referendum campaign plus some access to Dalyell's archives in the National Library of Scotland provide a much clearer picture of the extent of his daily involvement in the referendum campaign.[8]

Dalyell approached the 1979 devolution referendum with a clear letter-writing strategy. This strategy sought to exploit the letters pages of the press across all parts of Scotland, meaning in newspapers way beyond Dalyell's constituency to the West of Edinburgh – and in local papers not just *The Scotsman, The Herald, Daily Record*, etc., but also the *Alloa Advertiser, Falkirk Herald, Stirling Observer, Buchan Observer, Fife Free Press, The Shetland Times* and the *Stornoway Gazette* amongst others. There were two parts to the letter-writing campaign. First, Dalyell arranged for Scottish local newspapers to be sent to him at the House of Commons. Second, the idea was for Dalyell to write individualised letters on the devolution issue to a local paper. Rather than sending a standard letter to newspapers, Dalyell wrote individual replies to letters from other readers or from news stories, meaning that he was occasionally carrying out a dialogue with local people on the issues raised at the referendum. Dalyell explained the rationale for this approach in an interview in 2011:

> I did this because people actually read what is written in the local paper, often more carefully, than either the tabloid press or the broadsheets. And it was an avenue to just sew the seed of doubt in the minds of those who thought that devolution must be a good thing, that there were no drawbacks, that it was a relatively simple matter. And the letter writing campaign I conducted more or less like simultaneous chess. There were 82 local newspapers and I ordered the lot because you see Round Robin standardised letters would simply be spiked and quite rightly so. If on the other hand one could write to the John O' Groats Journal in relation to what Mrs McGinty

of John O' Groats had said last week then they were much more likely to print it. In fact I think I am right in saying that only two of my numerous letters were rejected because they were tagged on to something that had been written in the newspaper the week before or two weeks before. However tenuous the link might be, as long as there was a link editors were happy to use it. And I talked to quite a number of them and they sort of smiled at me and said 'You cunning bastard, but it filled our space and we thought that it was a legitimate thing for us to print'. And of course once the first letter appeared almost sure as nuts there would be a response, and of course that was gold dust as far as I was concerned. I could then respond again (SPA/745).

For example, in a response to a letter in *The Shetland Times*, Dalyell appealed to Shetlanders to vote No:

To David Robertson of Blairgowrie (*The Shetland Times*, 26th January) who attacks me on various grounds, I simply reply that on March 1st, the gut issue is whether people living in Scotland and Shetland wish to remain part of Britain. Those of us who do want to remain part of Britain must take the trouble to go out and vote since the 40 percent is only advisory to the House of Commons. If the 40 percent is not reached the House of Commons will decide, and in doing so will take into account the size of the No vote. So if Shetlanders feel No, they must go out whatever the weather as the size of the No vote is vital, and for all sorts of reasons the Shetland vote, counted separately, will be the subject of worldwide interest (*The Shetland Times*, 9th February 1979: 3).

Dalyell picked a quite different theme in a letter to the *Stornoway Gazette*:

I read with interest on page 1 of last week's Gazette that the Western Isles Liberal Association wants a Constitutional Court in this country.
Superficially it is an attractive proposal, but does it not have the same difficulties as the highly questionable notion in the Scotland Act that the inevitable rows, disputes and conflicts between the

47

High School in Edinburgh and the Scottish Cabinet on one side
and the British Government on the other, can be settled by the
Judicial Committee on the Privy Council?

The settlement of grounds about money and resources should
be part of the political process and not handed over to lawyers,
however distinguished!

The only way to avoid the conflict is to go out and Vote No
on March 1, and in sufficient numbers to defeat the costly
and dangerous Scotland Act (*Stornoway Gazette*, 6th January
1979: 6).

In a different way Dalyell sought to appeal to Labour voters and trade
union members to vote No in a letter to the *Buchan Observer* – part
of Labour Vote No's strategy to mobilise opposition from within the
Labour movement but tailored to suit a rural constituency:

Sir- your correspondent Alex Fleming says in a letter to you,
Observer 16th January, that the opposition to an Assembly in
Edinburgh is big business. He is right to the extent that most
manufacturers have become extremely worried about the
consequences and costs of devolution, but Mr Fleming only gives
part of the story.

Many full time trade union officials, up and down Scotland with
heavy responsibilities for the employment of their members are
equally opposed to an Assembly and are giving support to the
Labour Vote No campaign.

Ten years ago some 9,200,000 people were employed in
productive industry in Britain. Today the figure is around
7,800,000. Together with agriculture they form the base which
provides the bread and butter for the rest of us.

Should we really be adding yet another layer of government for,
stripped of the emotion, this is precisely what an Assembly is - to
our already overburdened industry and farming.

It is absurd for Mr Fleming to claim in your columns that if
there is a 'No' vote there will be little Scottish owned industry
to decide to go or stay. On the contrary since a 'Yes' vote will
sooner or later lead to frontiers, and since many firms have a
policy (Like IBM for example) of manufacturing where their

market is, it would be all too possible that decision to invest, which might have benefited Scotland, will be made with a view to where the market is – south of the border. If you are concerned and want jobs, go out and vote No (*Buchan Observer*, 30th January 1979: 6).

Finally, in a letter to the *Fife Free Press*, Dalyell uses the 'slippery slope' example that devolution will lead to independence as an argument for voting No at the referendum:

Sir, P C Walters in his letter, *Fife Free Press*, January 19th, suggests that 'those of us who are stomping round the country telling us we are 'not fit to govern ourselves' are 'defeatists' who should be 'slammed'.

Not so, the issue is not whether we are capable of governing ourselves, we are. The issue on March 1 is whether we wish to set in train a process which will lead to the break up of the British state and frontiers with England.

Those like Mr Walters who think for 2½ centuries they have lived under the dictat of an alien government had better vote yes on March 1, and for the SNP thereafter, the real leaders of the Yes campaign.

The rest of us, not a whit less patriotic than Mr Walters would be well advised not least in the light of outpourings by the SNP, to 'get up from our hunkers' as Mr Walters puts it, and vote no. The 40 percent is only advisory to the House of Commons and the actual size of the No vote will be crucial (*Fife Free Press*, 2nd February 1979: 14).

The extent of the letter-writing was evident from material in Dalyell's archive boxes in the NLS. For example, on 1st January 1979, Dalyell wrote to the *Hamilton Advertiser, Glasgow Herald* and *Dundee Courier*. On the 13th January, he wrote to the *Inverness Courier, Argyll Courier, Milngavie and Bearsden Herald, Ayrshire Post, Perthshire Advertiser, Arbroath Herald, Kilmarnock Standard* and the *Buteman*. On the 21st January, he wrote to the *Falkirk Herald, Alloa Advertiser, Kelso Chronicle* and *Jedburgh Gazette*. We have produced extracts of four letters above from the *Buchan Observer, Fife Free Press, The Shetland Times* and

Stornoway Gazette – though Dayell wrote a total of 11 letters to these papers during the campaign. And, this very personal campaign continued throughout the referendum campaign across many local and national newspapers.

The Speaking Tours

Public meetings and speaking tours were a key aspect of the 1979 referendum campaign and Dalyell was a prominent actor in this aspect of the campaign. Dalyell spoke in a variety of forums, sometimes on his own, sometimes with other speakers such as Jim Sillars – who held a large number of Yes versus No debates across Scotland. Some of Dalyell's speeches were to Labour and trade union organisations though, as we can see below, he travelled much more widely than this. He was not alone in undertaking such engagements. Opponents of devolution such as Conservative Teddy Taylor, Labour's George Cunningham, Church of Scotland Minister Andrew Herron, as well as Lord Wilson, Douglas Hardie and John Risk of Scotland Says No were also active in speaking at a variety of events during the campaign (NLS Acc 12918). Dalyell's list of speaking engagements from his archive boxes for January 1979 give some idea of his level of activity during the referendum:

- 3rd January – speech to local NFU at Oatridge Agricultural College, West Lothian.
- 7th January – debate with Jim Sillars at Maybole in Ayrshire.
- 8th January - debate with Martin O'Neill in Sauchie, Clackmannanshire.
- 11th January – spoke at Motherwell Civic Centre with George Cunningham and at NUPE trade union meeting at Bangour Hospital in West Lothian.
- 12th January – speech at Edinburgh Townswoman's Guild.
- 14th January - debate with Iain McCormick at Jewish Literary Society in Edinburgh.
- 17th January – debate with Jim Sillars in Aberdeen.
- 19th January – debate with Jim Sillars in Cumnock.

- 21st January – spoke at West Lothian Labour Party and at trade union meeting.
- 23rd January - debate with Duncan Milligan in Edinburgh.
- 24th January – debate with Jim Sillars at Glasgow College of Technology
- 26th January - talk at North British Steel foundry in Bathgate
- 30th January - Inverness Labour Party talk
- 31st January – debate with Jim Sillars in Hamilton.

Dalyell himself was very positive about the public meetings and particularly the meetings held with Jim Sillars:

> The organisation and structure of Labour Vote No was haphazard in the extreme. The public meetings were few and far between other than the 18 debates between me and Jim Sillars. It came about because we were the only two on the left who publicly felt passionately about it. Now Jim is a friend of mine... I have always liked him and I worked very hard for him at his by-election in March 1970 in South Ayrshire. We had such a good result that it made Harold Wilson go to the country earlier than he should have done with catastrophic results. Jim was a good friend but on the other hand we disagreed vehemently on this subject. Both of us had a lot to say on the matter. And my recollection is that it started with a debate in Bellshill and we realised that this worked very well and a lot of people were interested. The poster which showed both of us as boxers. These posters were put up in red and yellow showing Jim and I in red and yellow. It went up in the post offices and everything else. It attracted a great number of people because they thought that there would be great old fisticuffs. In a sense the campaign was Dalyell versus Sillars with everybody else sitting in the stalls (SPA/754).

Jim Sillars, 10.01 and The Margo Mobile in 2014

Whilst Tam Dalyell had retired from active politics by the time of independence referendum (he was 82), Jim Sillars hadn't (despite being 76). Indeed, the referendum gave Sillars a new lease of political life and, along with his wife Margo MacDonald, he was highly active during various stages of the campaign. Following Margo's death on 4th April 2014, Sillars became even more active, with a reprise of his speaking tour from 1979. This time, the tour did not involve Dalyell or any opponents, but instead a series of Yes supporters, through a large number of housing schemes in Scotland by day, with public meetings by night. Sillars had a small team of people working with him and utilized both traditional methods and new technology for the campaign: he also became a frequent tweeter and retweeter to promote the independence message.[9] He was central to three different but interlocking Yes campaigns: the 10.01 campaign, Nae Fear and the Margo Mobile, all promoted through social media and traditional campaigning. During the early parts of the long campaign, Sillars was a critical supporter of a Yes vote, often departing from the positions held by the SNP, Scottish Government and Yes Scotland. He was prominent in the *Options for Scotland* website (http://www.optionsforscotland.com), with former SNP leader Gordon Wilson. The website published dissenting pieces on currency, EU membership, defence, the tactics of the campaign, etc., from a range of authors. Some of the ideas discussed there fed into his book, *In Place of Fear II: A Socialist Programme for an Independent Scotland*, published in January 2014 (Sillars 2014): a clear echo of Nye Bevan's work of 1952. The book led to the 10.01 campaign through its expression of Scottish voter sovereignty for a short time on referendum day itself:

> On 18th September, 2014, between the hours of 7am and 10pm, absolute sovereign power will lie in the hands of the Scottish people. They have to decide whether to keep it, or give it away to where their minority status makes them permanently powerless and vulnerable.
> Without sovereignty, Scotland is inherently weakened. Oil, gas, energy, whisky, land and other vital national interests are externally owned, often by those who do not put Scotland's interests first. Without the power to intervene in the national interest, a power available through independence, not devolution, we are at the mercy of forces that have no concern for us, our welfare or our future.
> Independence alone can remedy this.[10]

The book was published on 20th January 2014, followed by appearances on STV's *Scotland Tonight* and BBC Question Time from Dundee. From then on until the end of August, Sillars was promoting the book, along with the independence message generally, across Scotland. From 5th February, the book gave birth to the 10.01 Campaign and tour, which began to promote the absolute sovereignty of Scottish voters on referendum day.[11] He started in Edinburgh, where he lives, and from there went on to Airdrie, West Calder, Govan in Glasgow, Inverness, Fort William, Shettleston in Glasgow, Edinburgh University, Ayr, Edinburgh again, New Cumnock, Edinburgh, Motherwell, Edinburgh and Renfrew on 3rd April.[12] At that stage, his wife, Margo MacDonald died, which led to the cancellation of a number of scheduled events. Margo had been one of the SNP's most prominent figures since the 1970s. Like Sillars, she had been elected as MP for Glasgow Govan at a by-election, had risen to a senior position within the party and also had major differences with it. She became a MSP in 1999 but was then re-elected as an independent MSP on the Lothians regional list from 2003 onwards. The couple had married in 1981 and she had proven a strong, recognizable and independent voice for independence during the referendum campaign: she was one of the few Scottish politicians to be known by her first name alone.

Following a large, public funeral, Sillars returned to campaigning in Wester Hailes in Edinburgh on 25th April and the book tour continued in Glasgow, Kirkintilloch, Kilmarnock, Annan, Glasgow Govan and a host of other locations from May to July.[13] At that stage, a new campaign initiative was launched by Jim Sillars – using the Margo Mobile, a specially converted bus fitted with a public address system, to tour Scotland promoting a Yes vote.[14] The Margo Mobile received two tranches of crowdfunding in July and August. The first crowdfunder sought to generate £50,000 but got just £18,600 from 376 people when it closed on 13th August 2014.[15] The second round of crowdfunding managed to raise £10,858 out of a target of £10,000 funded by 147 supporters by 30th August 2014.[16] The money went on the bus, repairs to the bus as well as diesel for the large amounts of travel involved (the 10.01 campaign as a whole spent £36,429.20 on transport from a total spend of £75,750.95).[17]

The Margo Mobile was launched in Govan on 5th August and from then, it combined speaking/campaign tours of housing schemes across Scotland with public meetings in the evenings to promote a Yes vote. The *In Place of Fear* website gives some indication of the evening meetings – though there were more than listed – but the bus tours were much more numerous. They would involve the bus meeting a group of activists, visiting several areas of high density housing (flats in council housing schemes often), where Sillars would make a short speech through the public address system and talk to voters. For example, take 29th August, when the Margo Mobile toured Ballingry, Cardenden, Glenrothes, Kirkcaldy and Lochgelly in Fife during the day, before visiting Dundee in the evening for a public meeting; or 18th August, when Sillars toured Bannockburn, Cultenhove and the Raploch in Stirling, followed by Falkirk and Grangemouth, before Prestonpans and Tranent in the evening. Or the tour of Broomhouse, Muirhouse, Oxgangs and Wester Hailes in Edinburgh on 15th August. Large parts of Ayrshire, Glasgow, Lanarkshire and Renfrewshire were covered by the Margo Mobile, touring towns, villages and housing estates pretty much every day from 5th August to the 16th September.[18] The tour was promoted through Facebook and twitter, featured a range of Yes groups and prominent supporters and concentrated on areas with older, working class, Labour voters who would be sympathetic to Sillars' message: he had first been elected as a Labour MP for South Ayrshire in 1970 and several tours took place in his former constituency. The Margo Mobile tour was extensive and not unlike the efforts of the Radical Independence Campaign and a number of local Yes groups, who targeted working class areas. The combined Nae Fear/10.01 Campaign/Margo Mobile also crowdfunded a number of pro-independence newspaper adverts, which raised £33,493 by 270 people in 15 days for 4 full-page national newspaper adverts.[19] Whereas time and technology meant that Tam Dalyell practiced a very traditional type of campaign, as well as a highly effective one, Sillars' campaign married traditional campaign techniques to social media promotion and fundraising. Though, its target was actually older traditional Labour voters who did not use social media, so its adoption of quite traditional techniques on the ground was deliberately chosen to reach its audience.

Conclusion

We can draw three broad conclusions from examining some of the literature and features of campaigns and campaigning. First, the literature on political campaigning has generally indicated professionalizing trends in modern campaigning, from traditional modes of campaigning to use of TV, political marketing and the use of the internet. We will find a very full menu of such campaign practices and styles across the three referendums featured in this book and, in particular, we will see some very rich campaign repertoires in 2014 by a range of actors: with practices as old school as they are ultra-modern. Second, referendum campaigns feature a range of political actors and organisations. Parties and governments are central – and governments are never 'neutral' at referendums in the UK – at both the national and local levels, as are business and trade union organisations and a range of civic groups. As we shall see, that was particularly strong feature of the 2014 independence referendum. But, even then, they had to register as campaign groups and play by the rules, just like the official umbrella campaign groups accorded official designation by the Electoral Commission. Finally, whilst much of this chapter focused on types of campaigning and the role of parties and umbrella groups, there is a role for individuals in referendum campaigning albeit in very different ways. The activities of Tam Dalyell at the 1979 devolution referendum showed the traditional but innovative manner in which a prominent MP campaigned against his own party, across Scotland through extensive letter-writing and speaking tours. His counterpart and main sparring partner from 1979, Jim Sillars, combined some of the traditional approaches of 1979, with the new social media techniques of 2014, through crowdfunding and promoting his campaign through social media. New campaign techniques and technology could therefore provide useful tools for single campaigners, not just political parties and campaign groups.

Endnotes

1.	Plus more advanced modeling and creation of voter types via Facebook by companies like Cambridge Analytica that have worked for the Brexit and Trump campaigns in more complex ways than were practiced at the 2014 independence referendum.

2.	Better Together also spent £8,958.26 on advertising and support services from Blue State Digital during the official campaign.

3.	See for example https://www.theguardian.com/commentisfree/2017/jun/28/paid-leave-vote-funding-brexit-public-inquiry and https://www.theguardian.com/news/2018/mar/18/cambridge-analytica-and-facebook-accused-of-misleading-mps-over-data-breach

4.	See https://www.channel4.com/news/topic/election-expenses

5.	There is also an ongoing study of 6 UK party memberships by the Tim Bale, Paul Webb and Monica Poletti funded by the ESRC see https://esrcpartymembersproject.org

6.	There is more recent membership data on the SNP after the surge in members that followed on from the independence referendum. However, whilst it revealed demographic patterns of the members, it didn't say anything about levels of activism amongst the new members. See Rob Johns and James Mitchell (2016), *Takeover: Explaining the Extraordinary Rise of the SNP*, London: Biteback.

7.	This was not a short-term process, but part of a longer term period of decline covered by Hassan and Shaw, 2012.

8.	Tam Dalyell's personal papers are lodged in Acc.12918, National Library of Scotland.

9.	See https://twitter.com/naefear

10.	http://www.inplaceoffear.com

11.	https://twitter.com/1001Campaign.

12.	http://www.inplaceoffear.com/in-place-of-fear-ii-book-tour/

13.	http://www.inplaceoffear.com/in-place-of-fear-ii-book-tour/

14.	http://www.margomobile.com

15.	https://www.indiegogo.com/projects/margo-mobile#/story

16.	https://www.indiegogo.com/projects/margo-mobile--2#/story

17.	10.01 campaign spending returns at the Electoral Commission for the regulated period of the 2014 referendum campaign.

18.	https://twitter.com/margomobileyes

19.	https://www.indiegogo.com/projects/indy-adverts#/story

3

The 1979 Devolution Referendum

Introduction

Referendums and referendum campaigns can have many similarities but they also have their own distinctive economic and political settings. For example, the 1979 devolution referendum was very different to later referendums in many respects. It occurred in a period in which referendums were new, novel and contested in UK politics. Referendums were seen as highly exceptional – with only two examples of the Northern Ireland sovereignty referendum of 1973 and the European Community referendum of 1975 before it. Even then, the Northern Ireland poll had experienced a Nationalist boycott that undermined its legitimacy. The political environment of the 1970s was also very different to today in relation to parties, party positions and campaigning. However, as we shall see, it was also very different to the second devolution referendum of 1997. First, there was the very different level of media available at the time of the first devolution referendum. The 1979 referendum took place before the internet – so no webpages, twitter, podcasts – but also in the period when there were only three TV channels (Channel 4 did not appear until 1982). There were also next to no computers (not as we know them now anyway), no mobile phones, no telephone canvassing, and none of the modern campaigning techniques of recent years that have utilised technology (direct mail for example): it can appear as the antithesis of the 2014 campaign. Campaigning was therefore quite traditional and involved pen and paper, leaflets, posters, public meetings, press releases to newspapers, limited TV coverage, etc.: though many of these traditional techniques would be in evidence from 2012 to 2014 too. We can find evidence of this kind of traditional campaigning in the use of the local newspapers in the referendum, particularly in things like letter-writing by campaigners discussed in chapter 2. Also, the referendum campaign did not have any party election broadcasts or even an information leaflet on devolution from the government – due to political divisions on the issue and a legal challenge by No campaigners to stop any election broadcasts (Fowler 1981: 122-7).

Second, and in common with 1997, campaigning itself was unregulated compared to now - the Electoral Commission did not exist - with no spending limits for the campaign or any public accountability over campaign spending: this latter point made it impossible to determine accurately how much money had been spent on the campaign by the different campaign groups. Bochel, Denver and Macartney's book on the 1979 referendum estimated that the combined Yes campaign spent something like £63,000, whilst the No campaign spent around £112,000 (Bochel, Denver and Macartney 1981: 30), with the spending divided between campaign materials, staffing, offices, etc. Scotland Says No had the larger resources and spent much more widely on poster sites and newspaper advertising (Bochel, Denver and Macartney 1981: 34).

Third, politics in 1979 was different compared to now, though some aspects of it remain important (the centrality and bitterness of the Labour-SNP conflict for example). Labour was much more ideological as a political force and also highly divided on devolution – some of this was down to ideology, some down to hatred of the Nationalists and also due to opposition to being seen to cave-in to Nationalist pressure to create a Scottish Assembly at all. Enthusiasm for devolution within Labour was also seen to be quite limited. As Vernon Bogdanor commented after the 1979 referendums:

> the Scotland and Wales Acts were born, not out of a principled belief in the dispersal of power from Whitehall, but from expediency. Few in the Labour Party, with the honourable exception of the late John Mackintosh, cared for devolution for its own sake. Indeed,

one advisor to the government assured me that only one and a half members of the Wilson Cabinet had been in favour of devolution, the one being Mr William Ross, a late enthusiastic convert, the half being Sir Harold himself (Paterson 1998: 132).

Labour itself had only won the October 1974 general election narrowly and its tiny Westminster majority of three seats fell away until it was a minority government reliant on the Liberals to remain in office: hence the Lib-Lab pact that began in March 1977. This political reality had a serious effect on the devolution issue. It meant that Labour struggled to construct a parliamentary majority for its devolution proposals at Westminster, and left it at the mercy of its own backbenchers (meaning Labour's devo-sceptics such as Tam Dalyell, George Cunningham, Robin Cook, etc.), the Conservative opposition and House of Lords as well as the Liberals and SNP. The result was that Labour lost control of the devolution issue at Westminster and was forced to amend its legislative proposals to suit party dissidents – this resulted in the necessity of holding a referendum to implement the Scotland Act 1978 as well as the 40 per cent rule: that 40 per cent of the registered electorate would need to vote Yes to devolution for the Assembly to be created (Bogdanor, 1996). Furthermore, such divisions did not only exist in the Houses of Parliament, they were evident on the ground in the Labour Party at the referendum itself as we shall see.

Fourth, the SNP, though founded in 1934, was a very new force at Westminster. The party's electoral success in 1974 had brought 11 MPs to Westminster but also pushed the devolution issue up the political agenda – not least as the SNP threatened so many Labour seats in Scotland (the party had 36 second places to Labour in October 1974). However, the devolution issue was very controversial within the SNP, with the party divided on the issue and worried about the impact of the issue on the party's electoral prospects. In addition, by the time the referendum was held, support for the SNP was on the slide – it had peaked in opinion polls in March 1977 on 36 per cent,[1] but its poll ratings declined during 1978. In this period, the party performed badly at elections to Regional Councils in May 1978, coming third with 20.9 per cent and also lost out to Labour in the three crucial by-elections of Glasgow Garscadden, Hamilton and Berwick and East

Lothian (Wilson 2009). The Scotland bill passed its third reading in the House of Commons in February 1978, before being enacted on 31st July 1978: which also took the political steam out of the SNP.

Finally, the Conservatives were a much stronger force in Scottish politics in 1979 than at the two subsequent referendums. Moreover, the party was involved in a rather different referendum campaign than the others. It was somewhat divided on devolution, with a number of key figures actually supportive of the Assembly however, it was focused on winning the UK general election and returning to power at Westminster: and this involved seeing Labour and the SNP damaged by the devolution issue. The Tories managed their divisions on devolution extremely well – and did so from the top through Mrs Thatcher's careful handling of devolution in the early years of her leadership (Torrance 2009) - and adopted a cautious approach during the campaign to avoid hurting their electoral prospects if there was a strong Yes vote. In a memo to local party chairmen, Scottish Tory President Russell Sanderson carefully explained the party's position:

> The Party would campaign for a "No" vote on the understanding that some members may wish to vote "Yes".......Let me make it quite clear that in campaigning for "No", the Party will not be campaigning against Devolution for Scotland but only against the type of devolution contained in the Act. In the event of the "no" campaign being successful, the Party is committed to the establishment of an all-Party conference to discuss better forms of Devolution........... Lastly, let me remind you that it is fully appreciated that there are loyal members of the Party who hold sincere views opposed to the "No" campaign. They must feel free to pursue these views during the Referendum, and we must never forget our prime objective is to win the forthcoming general election which may follow very quickly after March 1st (Denver, Bochel and Macartney 1981: 22-3).

Economic and Political Context

Referendums do not occur in a vacuum. They occur at certain times, usually for very specific political reasons. In some countries, referendums are required because of their constitution and whether a political change domestically or internationally will effectively amend a country's constitution – such as treaty changes by the European Union. However, in the UK, party preferences and issues of party management are influential in referendums, not the constitution. UK referendums occur through government choice, mostly on a timetable the government prefers, to serve party interests. However, the 1979 devolution does not entirely fit this picture, as it was forced on a minority Labour Government by its own backbenchers and the opposition, who also created the requirement that 40 per cent of the registered electorate would need to vote for devolution for it to be instituted (the 40 per cent rule). This scenario still left the government in charge of the devolution question and the timing of the referendum to some extent, but it would be hard to argue that Labour was able to hold the referendum in a favourable environment which would create the 'winning conditions' for a Yes vote to devolution. In this sense, neither the political or economic context was helpful to proponents of constitutional change in 1979 (even though there was actually a Yes vote at the conclusion of the campaign).

The Political Context

The period leading up to the 1979 referendum was a paradoxical one for Labour in Scotland and in the UK. The party had been under pressure since the February 1974 general election in both Scotland and at Westminster. This pressure exhibited itself through election results as well as opinion poll ratings, not least as the Labour government saw its Westminster majority disappear and faced serious economic problems throughout its term in office. Despite this, Labour's performance from 1974-9 was not all negative. It faced a number of by-elections in this period and lost some significant ones, but there was nothing apocalyptic about its performance. For example, the party faced seven by-elections in 1977, four in seats that it held and it retained two and lost two (in Birmingham Stechford as Roy Jenkins became President of the European Commission and in Ashfield as sitting MP David Marquand resigned to become Jenkin's advisor). The Birmingham result was significant as it marked the by-election at which Labour lost its majority in the House of Commons – on 31st March. From then on, working through parliament was even more problematic. In 1978, eight of the ten UK by-elections occurred in Labour-held seats, yet the party lost only one and held seven. In terms of opinion polls, Labour's performance fluctuated, though with ratings that subsequent leaders of the party would have killed for. For example, significant Tory opinion poll leads throughout most of 1977 had evaporated by October and Labour became much more competitive with the Tories from then until the early months of 1979. Opinion polls saw small leads for either party as well as a dead heat at 43.5 per cent each in a Gallup poll for the *Daily Telegraph* on 15th May 1978 and again on 45.5 per cent each on 12th June 1978. Labour led in the first opinion poll of 1979, with 49.1 per cent to 42.5 per cent, but from then on, economic and political conditions deteriorated and there was a Conservative lead from then to the general election, except for a 0.9 per cent lead for Labour in a GOP poll for the *Daily Mail* on 30th April 1979.[2] Notably, Labour lost the 1979 general election, seeing its vote decline to 36.9 per cent (-2.3 per cent), whilst the new Conservative government was elected with 43.9 per cent (+8.1 per cent) and the Liberals fell to 13.8 per cent.

In Scotland, whilst there were fluctuations in support, Labour's position in opinion polls was healthier. For example, whilst support for the party was dented by the popularity of the SNP and the Conservatives in 1976 and 1977, as each party would poll around a third of the vote, Labour's position stabilized into 1978. The party saw its vote grow from 34 per cent in January 1978 to a high of 52 per cent in August, as SNP support slumped to 18 per cent and the Conservatives to 24 per cent. Though Conservative support recovered, the SNP didn't and Labour enjoyed strong polling leads through the referendum to the general election.[3] The 1979 general election was cataclysmic for the SNP as it lost nine of its eleven MPs and saw its vote drop to 17.3 per cent (-13.1 per cent). Labour was the clear beneficiary as its vote rose to 41.5 per cent (+5.2 per cent), but so were the Conservatives, as they recovered seats from the SNP and saw their vote rise to 31.4 per cent (+6.7 per cent). The first past the post system helped Labour to win 41 seats (one more than

October 1974), whilst the number of Conservative seats increased by eight to twenty two.

Opinion poll ratings aren't everything but they did indicate some of the main electoral developments in Scotland in the year leading up to the devolution referendum on 1st March 1979. For example, in Scotland, Labour faced regional council elections in May 1978 as well as what could have been a tricky series of by-elections against the SNP. At the first by-election in Glasgow Garscadden on 13th April 1978, Labour's Donald Dewar held the seat, despite losing 5.5 per cent support since the October 1974 general election and the SNP vote was only marginally higher at 32.9 per cent. Labour's position was reinforced by its position at the regional elections, where its vote increased to 39.6 per cent (an increase of 8 per cent from the district council elections the previous year), the Conservatives saw an increase in support to 30.3 per cent and the SNP declined to third place on 20.9 per cent. These changing fortunes were evident at the Hamilton by-election on 31st May, when Labour actually increased its level of support from October 1974 by 2.5 per cent whilst the SNP declined 5.6 per cent to come second with 33.4 per cent of the vote, despite the presence of the charismatic and popular Margo MacDonald in the by-election seat famously won by Winnie Ewing back in 1967. The third in the series of by-elections was even better for Labour, as it retained the Berwick and East Lothian seat by increasing its support with 47.4 per cent over the Conservatives on 40.2 per cent as the SNP was squeezed out and saw its vote decline to 8.8 per cent.

Public attitudes to devolution during this period also reveal the political context of the referendum, especially as they illustrated changing public attitudes on the issue. Bochel, Denver and Macartney's 1979 referendum study covered both short-term and longer-term attitudes to constitutional change in general in addition to opinion on the Labour Government's devolution proposals. Opinion polls on support for different constitutional options from 1975 to 1979 sought to determine opinion on devolution, independence and the constitutional status quo: similar options featured in polling for several decades after. However, some of the polls in the sequence were complicated by the fact that the devolution option was not a single option, but a bundle of 2-3 devolution alternatives. So, ORC's June 1975 poll found support for independence at 20 per cent and for the status quo at 22 per cent, but whilst the devolution option was clearly the most popular on 58 per cent, it involved 3 broad 'change' alternatives derived from polling for the Royal Commission on the Constitution (see Kellas 1989: 148). Once polling settled down to concentrate on sampling attitudes to the Labour Government's devolution proposals against other firm options then attitudes became slightly clearer. MORI's polls in December 1976 put support for devolution at 55 per cent, with 21 per cent for the status quo and 23 per cent for independence. In April 1978, the picture for MORI was little changed, with 54 per cent support for devolution, 26 per cent for the status quo and 21 per cent for independence (Macartney 1981: 32). In all polls during the period, devolution in its various forms was always the most popular option, but support for the status quo grew stronger and that for independence declined in some polls. For example, into 1979, support for the status quo was registering from 29-37 per cent, with independence peaking at 26 per cent but falling to 12 per cent after the devolution referendum of 1st March (Macartney 1981: 32). On the day itself, ORC's poll put devolution on 45 per cent, the status quo on 29 per cent and independence on 26 per cent. However, these 3 options had to be squeezed into a binary choice and produced only a small margin in favour of devolution. The devolution and independence supporters had not coalesced to produce a convincing Yes majority for change on the day.

With attitudes to devolution itself, support was very high in 1976 and 1977, with ORC's October 1976 poll putting Yes on 80 per cent and No on 20 per cent and a further ORC poll in February 1977 putting Yes on 78 per cent to 22 per cent for No. Similar polls for System 3, MORI and PSL gave smaller but still commanding leads for Yes from 1976-78 (Macartney 1981: 32). However, into 1979, the polls tightened considerably. System 3 placed the Yes-No balance at 64-36 per cent on 20th January 1979, changing to 56-44 per cent on 6th February and then to 52-48 per cent on 25th February. The Yes-No balance for MORI shifted from 64-36 per cent on 14th February to 60-40 per cent on 22nd February and then to 50-50 on 28th February (Macartney 1981: 32). ORC's polls were more optimistic for Yes, with a 61-39 per cent balance on 20th February and then a 57-43 per cent balance on 1st March itself (Macartney 1981: 32). However, the actual result was a very narrow 51.6 per cent for Yes to 48.4 per cent for No.

The economic context for the 1979 devolution referendum was poor, even if some of the statistics from the time do not appear so bad in a longer term perspective. So, unemployment at the time appeared relatively small compared to what was to follow in the 1980s, but it was much higher than previously experienced in the post-war years of growth, when unemployment was negligible. In early 1974, UK unemployment was 3.6 per cent, rising to 5.3 per cent in early 1976 and then remained above 5 per cent through the period to the referendum:[4] accompanied by other economic problems, this helped to create a negative backdrop at the referendum and in politics generally. Annual levels of inflation increased from 16 per cent in 1974 to peak at 24.2 per cent in 1975 before falling down to 8.3 per cent in 1978,[5] just in advance of the referendum. Interest rates moved from 11.4 per cent in 1975 to 9 per cent in 1978 and then upward to 13.7 per cent by the end of 1979.[6]

A considerable conditioning factor at the referendum was a series of industrial disputes over pay levels in 1978 and 1979, influenced by a UK government pay policy that sought to keep public sector wage increases below 5 per cent to reduce inflation. Lorry and tanker drivers went on strike in late 1978 and early 1979, which meant that oil and petrol supplies were disrupted (in winter) and all sorts of other road transport of goods was effected. The broader set of strikes known as the Winter of Discontent began on 3rd January 1979 – a series of national strikes for a month by lorry drivers, ambulance drivers and everyone from gravediggers to dustmen. According to Yes campaign participant and SNP member Isobel Lindsay,

> Had the referendum taken place in the autumn, rather than the spring, things might have been different. By the time of the referendum, in the event, there had been the winter of discontent, the popularity of the government had slumped, there had been bad weather, bad politics, bad industrial relations, an atmosphere that all changes were for the worst (Kemp 1993: 129).

Dennis Canavan felt the impact of the economic situation and winter of discontent very directly amongst Labour supporters in his constituency during the referendum campaign:

It was not just council workers, National Health workers, gravediggers, you name it. There was rubbish piling up in the streets and rats and everything. People – even traditional Labour supporters – were saying, 'what the hell is going on here?'. The country is in absolute chaos and you are expecting us to go out and vote in a referendum, what has a referendum got to do with this? A lot of people, even traditional Labour supporters, would see the referendum as a way to give Jim Callaghan and his Government a bloody nose, or in fact, a fatal blow (SPA/158).

The National Campaign

The 1979 devolution referendum did not simply have Yes and No campaigns, in which political parties were clearly aligned. It had two umbrella groups – Yes for Scotland and Scotland Says No but also a range of other campaign groups and, on the Yes side, a definite problem of lack of cooperation and open conflict between Yes organisations. Yes for Scotland largely involved the SNP and Jim Sillars' breakaway Scottish Labour Party but failed to attract prominent supporters from other parties in order to widen its appeal – specifically Labour. The group wanted someone like pro-devolution Tory Alick Buchanan-Smith to become the leading figure but this did not transpire so that the main Yes umbrella organisation did not seem cross-party to any great extent. Leading Yes campaigner Jim Sillars was acutely aware of the problem here:

> Knowing that my presence meant no Labour MP would join, I tried to leave the Yes For Scotland campaign quietly......If I resigned in public, opponents would say the Yes side was falling apart (Sillars 1995: 65).

However, no such resignation was possible and the limited cross-party nature of Yes for Scotland remained and continued as a political problem. In addition, Labour formed its own Yes campaign, Labour Movement Yes, comprised of Labour and the trade unions. Labour's Scottish Secretary Helen Liddell sent an infamous memo to

Constituency Labour Parties setting out the reasons for a separate Labour campaign – which largely involved seeking to marginalise the SNP and emphasising that devolution was not independence – and she explained that:

> We will not be soiling our hands by joining any umbrella Yes group. We will be fighting for devolution only with the Scottish TUC and the Co-operative Party (Bochel, Denver and Macartney 1981: 17).

Another Yes campaign group – albeit one that never had any organisation on the ground – was the Alliance for an Assembly which was (re)created in November 1978 with Alick Buchanan-Smith of the Tories, Russell Johnston of the Liberal Party, Donald Dewar from Labour and James Milne from the Scottish Trades Union Congress. However, it seems to have had only symbolic importance in showing a level of cross-party support for the Assembly. Beside these organisations were the SNP Yes Campaign, the Conservative Yes Campaign and some local campaigning by the Liberal Party and the Communists (see Bochel, Denver and Macartney 1981: 14-20, for more information on the different Yes campaigns). The role of the Labour Party on the ground in the Yes campaign was a problematic one, with the role of local parties and activists compromised by opposition to devolution itself. Local parties and trades unions were central to Labour's efforts in the Yes campaign but delivering upon the numerical superiority of potential campaigners was difficult. *Scotsman* journalist Neil Ascherson's pre-referendum tour of Scotland found few signs of life. At Aberdeen Trades Council, Ascherson observed that:

> Through the locked glass door of each trades union office, piles of Yes leaflets and posters could be made out lying on the carpet – never to be distributed (Ascherson 2002: 103).

Some of the lack of activity in Aberdeen was down to Labour politics in the city. Whilst there were some active Yes campaigners in Aberdeen who found a positive cross-party environment in the city and around Aberdeenshire, the city's Labour MP – Bob Hughes in Aberdeen North – was opposed to devolution and that effected the campaign, even though some local trade union figures were actively in favour (Bob McLean SPA/774).

Money and organisation for the referendum campaign tilted strongly towards the No campaign even if the Yes campaign should have had more people on the ground to undertake campaigning. As Yes for Scotland campaigner Jim Sillars explained:

> The first worry was money. Yes for Scotland did not have any and I had to fund the first print of our leaflet, hoping it would sell well enough to pay me back and finance the next printing. It did sell and we finally printed and paid for one million. But it was an uphill struggle even when some individuals made, for them, quite substantial contributions. But we needed that money to cover telephones and the printing of other leaflets. It was a shoestring organisation, kept going by the sheer dedication of the many young people who worked themselves into the ground trying to match the well-financed, well-oiled No campaign (Sillars 1995: 66).

Moreover, the nature of the referendum campaign brought some unlikely cross-party alliances that helped finance campaigning efforts. According to *Scotsman* journalist Neil Ascherson, some of the activities of the Labour Vote No committee of Robin Cook, Tam Dalyell and Brian Wilson were funded by Conservative supporters. As Ascherson explained:

> Its poster sites were being rented for it by the Tory-backed tycoon-fronted group 'Scotland Says No; with money laundered through an anti-devolution trade union (Ascherson 2002: 95).

The lack of a Labour campaign did not deter some Yes supporters, who realised that mobilising Labour voters to support the Assembly was a vital part of the referendum campaign. As West Lothian Yes activist Stewart Stevenson explained:

> The Labour Party nationally was campaigning yes, but in West Lothian they were not campaigning. So Alex (Salmond) and I arranged to collect the leaflets and posters for the Labour Party and we ran a virtual Labour Party campaign on their behalf.[7]

Former Scottish Labour Party MP Jim Sillars continues this theme:

> Labour were actually playing a double game. Officially, it was in favour of a Yes vote but many MPs and leading activists, such as Brian Wilson, and constituency parties, were campaigning on the No side....This meant that Labour's official campaign stuttered and spluttered, gave no positive leadership and thus further weakened Scottish resolve. In fact, there were frequent occasions when SNP and SLP activists in the Yes for Scotland campaign quietly helped out the very small groups of Labour Yes activists by distributing thousands of official Labour leaflets (Sillars 1995: 65).

Having said that, Labour did function during the referendum, both nationally and locally, as did the other political parties. They organized postal votes, did leafleting, some canvassing, some public meetings etc, and distributed thousands of leaflets, posters, car stickers and badges (Macartney 1981: 33). So, despite the political constraints on the campaign – and some lack of enthusiasm to sit along side partisan divisions on devolution – there was a fair amount of political activity at the referendum itself, though nothing compared to what you'd expect to find at a general election.

Scotland Says No was the most prominent No campaign group. It involved both Conservative and Labour MPs and had its origins in the Scotland is British group formed in 1976 – this gave it an organisational head-start compared to the Yes campaign. This umbrella group had relaxed relations with people from different parties involved in the No campaign meaning that MPs would cooperate across the partisan divide even when there were also an official Conservative No campaign and the Labour Vote No Campaign, which focused on turning Labour supporters against devolution (see Bochel, Denver and Macartney 1981: 20-24, for more information on the different No campaigners). This group also had the benefit of being able to focus on two distinct targets in the referendum – campaigning for a No vote, but also raising questions and generating confusion to dissuade people from voting as these would count as No votes under the 40 per cent rule. Labour MP Tam Dalyell was prominent in this group and played an extremely active role in the campaign throughout. Labour itself was also quite divided on the devolution issue, with activists campaigning for the No side in some places or not campaigning at all.

Part of the No campaign's strategy was to focus on the negative aspects of devolution, reflecting themes and criticisms that would also emerge at the 1997 devolution referendum. According to Scotland is British in 1978:

> Devolution will mean: more taxes, more politicians, more civil servants, worse government, less influence in London, greater demands for the break-up of the country (Scotland is British, 1978).

Internal Conservative pamphlets at the time pointed out that the Assembly

> is regarded as inevitable, a sop to nationalism, another unnecessary tier of government, another bureaucracy, another talking shop, yet another set of elections to be fought (McLetchie and Forsyth 1975: 4).

Some local Conservatives struggled with the practical effects of a Scottish assembly. As former Stirling activist John Holliday pointed out:

> I could see the general appeal of a Scottish Parliament. But what's it for? was my approach. So I ended up deciding I was agin it so took part in the No campaign. I was against it because all I could see was that it would cost money and not achieve a lot (SPA/507).

But, the No campaign also sought to conflate devolution with independence – to play upon the fact that the SNP was in favour of devolution as a first step to independence. A Scotland is British campaign leaflet in 1978 stated that:

> Separation will mean – Scots-English alienation, economic disruption, less investment, fewer jobs (Scotland is British, 1978).

Whilst the Conservatives developed some consistent themes to deploy at the referendum, whilst carefully seeking to avoid becoming damaged through their opposition to devolution, Labour was in an entirely different position. Labour opposition to devolution was noticeable locally in terms of the level of campaigning at the referendum and in relations with other political campaigners – really meaning with their SNP competitors on the ground across Scotland. Indeed, separating devolution from hatred of the SNP seemed an insurmountable obstacle for many Labour activists (a continuing theme in Scottish political life). As Pro-devolution Labour MP Dennis Canavan explained:

> There was also an element in the Labour Party who adhered to the politics of blind reaction. In many parts of Scotland, Labour's main challengers were no longer the Tories but the SNP. During the 1970s, the SNP had control of several local councils covering parts of my constituency, including Falkirk, Strathkelvin and Cumbernauld and Kilsyth. As a result, many Labour Party activists, especially Labour councillors, saw the SNP as the enemy and they hated everything the SNP stood for. The SNP's fundamental goal is an independent Scotland and, in 1979, they saw Labour's devolution proposals as inadequate. Nevertheless, many SNP members saw devolution as a stepping-stone to independence and were therefore campaigning for a "Yes" vote at the referendum. That was enough for many Labour councillors and Labour activists to resort again to the politics of blind reaction. If the SNP was voting "Yes", we must vote "No" (Canavan 2009: 199).

Of course, the No campaign did not just utilise arguments against the Assembly in a negative way. The campaign also developed a new approach, demonstrated most clearly in Lord Home's broadcast that held out the prospect of a future Conservative government producing more effective devolution proposals than those contained in the Scotland Act 1978. As Neal Ascherson explained in an entry from his reporter's notebook at the time:

> The No side have no fresh arguments, or at least the four or five they laid down in December – cost, extra tier of government, more bureaucracy, "separation" – have stopped making converts; the Yes side is now demolishing these arguments. But, the "vote no and get a better Act ploy" is new....Mass defection to No by Labour Councillors,

regional and district....Many now work for the (Tory-run) "Scotland Says No". In their dim minds, this is less disloyal than working for Tam Dalyell and the "Labour Vote No" campaign (Ascherson 2002: 102).

The Local Campaign

Bochel, Denver and Macartney's referendum study examined local campaigning in general as well as the local press, whilst also focusing specifically on campaign activity in Aberdeen, Dundee, Edinburgh and Glasgow. The local campaigns were important as the different sides in the referendum sought to mobilise voters through normal party channels as well as *ad hoc* cross-party arrangements. As we will see below, efforts to mobilise the Labour electorate in particular was seen to be important – as the Labour vote plus the SNP electorate from 1974 would see the devolution legislation receive a Yes vote. For example, the combined vote in favour of the two parties at the October 1974 general election was 87.1 per cent in Clackmannan and East Stirlingshire, 83 per cent in Stirling, Falkirk and Grangemouth and 77.2 per cent in Stirlingshire West. Local campaign activity varied markedly both geographically and by party. Bochel and Denver (1981) surveyed local parties organizations to determine their involvement in the referendum campaign – to try to determine the level of campaign intensity at the referendum. For example, very few local referendum campaigns seemed to be at the same level as a general election, with many of them less than at a local election and some local parties reporting very little effort at all. For example, 46 per cent of active local Conservative organisations felt that their referendum effort was less than that of a local election – a view shared by 37 per cent of active Labour branches. Amongst Liberals, 42 per cent of active local parties felt there had been very little effort at the referendum at all. Amongst local SNP parties 56 per cent reported that they had campaigned more than at a local election but less than at a general election (Bochel and Denver 1981: 54).

Local newspapers plus the recollections of local campaigners are good mechanisms to try to reconstruct the level of campaigning that took place across Stirling, Falkirk and Clackmannanshire in the weeks leading up to the referendum. The three local newspapers in the area – the *Alloa Advertiser, Falkirk Herald* and *Stirling Observer* – all featured different aspects of the campaign such as press statements from MPs and councillors, notice of public meetings by Yes and No campaigners, coverage of public meetings and events and the letters pages of the papers often featured discussion of the devolution issue. The local papers featured New Year's messages from local MPs that looked ahead to the devolution referendum (*Stirling Observer*, 3rd January 1979: 7), as well as frequent Yes/No articles or press statements from the various campaigners throughout the campaign and a bagful of reader's letters from local campaigners as well as from prominent devolution campaigners like Tam Dalyell and George Cunningham. Out of the three different newspapers sampled here, the *Alloa Advertiser* and *Stirling Observer* took no editorial position on the referendum whilst the *Falkirk Herald* recommended a No vote on 1st March in its front-page article 'A time to say No':

> Of all the pointless exercises in which this Nation has indulged, surely Thursday's referendum must be among the silliest. All through this year we have been faced with the appalling industrial unrest, rising inflation, lost export orders and growing unemployment. At times the very survival of our society seems to have been threatened. Now instead of tacking the divisions in our midst, we are to be asked whether we want an Assembly in Edinburgh, over and above Westminster, the Regions and the Districts, which would make us the most over-governed nation on earth (*Falkirk Herald*, 24th February: 1).

At one level, all the MPs in the area were active campaigners for the Yes side: Dennis Canavan, Harry Ewing of Labour and George Reid of the SNP were prominent within the campaign. However, their influence on the campaign on the ground was not necessarily shared within their parties. As Dennis Canavan explained in his autobiography:

> In my own constituency the Kilsyth branch of the Labour Party declared itself opposed to devolution and, when I visited Kilsyth on referendum day, I was dismayed to see "Labour Vote No" posters

73

on display throughout the town. Labour councillor Tom Barrie, ironically a great Burns enthusiast, joined a parcel o' rogues who put more effort into the "Labour Vote No" campaign than they had put into Labour's previous general election campaign, when I was Labour candidate (Canavan 2009: 199).

In Clackmannanshire, the local Labour Party was not involved in the referendum campaign in an official capacity, so that Yes campaigners from the Labour and trade union movement worked through Clackmannanshire Trades Council to establish a Yes campaign group through a meeting in Fishcross Miners Welfare Club on 1st February (*Alloa Advertiser*, 26th January 1979: 5). The group held a number of public meetings during the campaign featuring MPs and trade union leaders, whilst Kincardine Labour Club funded a Yes advert in the *Alloa Advertiser* on 21st and 23rd February before the referendum itself (For a Better Scotland. Vote Yes). Labour supporters in the area included the party candidate Martin O'Neill and his election agent, but there was little to no cooperation between Labour and the SNP during the referendum campaign: indicative of the intense local rivalries between the two parties generated by the 1974 general elections as well as the impending Westminster contest in 1979.

Local government was also less than enthusiastic about devolution. Stirling District Council was run by the Conservatives and the Provost Laura McCaig took a critical approach to the Assembly proposal, that focused on the problems of local government dealing with the Assembly, the issue of over-government with two local authority tiers plus an Assembly and the difficulties of MPs and the secretary of State having no input into local government. McCaig's solution to the devolution issue was twofold:

> I think the work of the Scottish Grand Committee should be better publicised. Perhaps it could meet in Scotland. Then we could have ministers debating in public what they are doing. (*Stirling Observer*, 7th February 1979: 9).

This proposal later became part of the Conservatives response to demands for devolution in the 1990s, with the reform of the Scottish Grand Committee in the Taking Stock document in 1993 plus

Michael Forsyth's proposals in the mid-1990s. The Labour leader of Central Regional Council, James Anderson was also unenthusiastic about the Scottish Assembly, concerned about its negative effect on local government through taking on administrative functions from councils and centralising power in Edinburgh. Anderson was also worried that voters knew too little about the issue at the referendum:

> My fear is that people are not well enough informed. There should have been a major campaign to inform people what this is all about so they could have made a positive decision (*Stirling Observer*, 7th February 1979: 9).

Of course, such a public information campaign had been ruled out by the government due to internal opposition from Labour devosceptic MPs in 1978, with a perception amongst Yes campaigners that this was intended to lower turnout at the referendum (Bochel, Denver and Macartney 1981: 5). No campaigners had also blocked party political broadcasts on the issue by legal action shortly before referendum day itself (Fowler, 1981: 125). In any event, when Central Regional Council considered whether it should express its support for a Yes vote at the referendum, the proposal was defeated by 24 votes to 8, largely reflecting partisan voting between the pro-Yes SNP councillors and the other parties: it was the SNP that had proposed a Yes endorsement by the council (*Alloa Advertiser*, 16th February 1979: 3). By contrast, Clackmanannshire District council, which was controlled by the SNP, did endorse a Yes vote at the referendum, though this was opposed by the other political parties The SNP carried the day by 6 votes to 4, with the active opposition of Labour and Conservative councillors and one Labour Councillor criticising the SNP for bringing 'politics into the chamber' by proposing the motion (*Alloa Advertiser*, 21st February 1979: 1).

Whilst Labour was divided locally on the devolution issue so that its campaign efforts were hindered, the SNP was more active. Local MP George Reid was hyperactive during the referendum campaign, with an extensive series of public meetings, campaign events and use of the local newspapers: the question and answer section that featured regularly in the *Alloa Advertiser* was a good example.

Though the SNP endorsed a Yes vote at the referendum and ran local and national campaigns in support of a Yes vote, the party and its activists had considerable reservations over the campaign. As local SNP activist Ruth Marr explained in relation to the quality of the devolution proposals:

> We had campaigned so hard for years. We had had the Scotland's Oil campaign; we had got eleven MPs elected to Westminster. And I think we all sort of thought, well we can do better than this, you know. Is this what we have been working for? We should be getting something with teeth and I think we felt that it did not have the teeth. Although we were certainly going out to vote for it there wasn't the same enthusiasm as there was in 1997 (SPA/143/2).

Local SNP campaigner David Alexander had similar memories of the campaign in the Falkirk area:

> I was probably unique in Falkirk politics in the sense that I was about the only one who was 100 per cent behind the referendum campaign. It was my first campaign really. I had only been in the party a few months. What became obvious was that all the parties were either lukewarm or hostile. The SNP were quite divided locally as to should we be campaigning for a Labour compromise - as it looked at the time. There were suspicions that the Labour Party were going through the motions and that we would be blamed for the failure of the referendum campaign. So there was a strong opinion at that time within local SNP circles that we should not be as active in the campaign. We certainly should not lead it because we would be blamed for its failure because of the 40 per cent rule. And the fact that the wind was blowing in a different direction by that time. Our political opponents who should have been our allies during that campaign, the Liberals don't have an organisation in Falkirk. And the Labour party locally, despite Harry Ewing being the local referendum minister, the local Labour Party were 100 per cent against the proposed assembly and the Tories were as they have always been anti-devolution, anti-Scottish, against the establishment of any kind of Parliament or Assembly. It was a strange campaign to be involved in, the indifference of SNP activists and the absolute hostility of -

despite it being a Labour proposal - amongst the local Labour Party meant that it was quite a lonely campaign (SPA/161).

Though it was his first campaign, Alexander was involved in multiple campaign activities across Falkirk and Grangemouth – meaning door knocking and leafleting (despite a lack of active members), use of SNP leaflets and stickers rather than cross-party material as well as polling day duty to mobilise supporters, especially in the working class areas that the party had been active in. On the No side locally were the Conservatives. There was next to no sign of Liberal campaigning in the referendum campaign in the area, besides one letter to the *Falkirk Herald* from a former Liberal candidate in the area that opposed devolution and proposed a federal Europe instead (*Falkirk Herald*, 24th February 1979: 14).

One unexpected area that saw support for the devolution proposals came from Church of Scotland Ministers in the area. Though the Church had produced a statement on the devolution issue through its Church and Nation Committee that was seen to support devolution, dissenting Ministers had prevented the statement from being read out following a special Commission of the General Assembly. However, the Rev. John Harvey of St Mark's Church Raploch and Rev. Alistair Hunter of Viewfield both read out the Kirk's statement on devolution to their congregations as part of their sermons on the Sunday before the referendum, to the consternation of opponents of a Scottish Assembly in the church: making front page news the day before the referendum was held (*Stirling Observer*, 28th February 1979: 1).

In addition, though the trade unions were formally in favour of a Scottish Assembly, with many active in the Yes campaign, this support was by no means solid as this letter from the chair of Central Scotland's Amalgamated Union of Engineering Workers made clear:

> It is a matter of regret to us, as supporters of much of the Labour Government's policies to find ourselves in opposition on this particular issue - but is our strongly held view that a separate Scottish Assembly cannot be justified administratively, economically, industrially or indeed, on any grounds other than politically as a sop to a nationalistic emotion - and on

77

that basis would be simply yet another unnecessary, and costly, bureaucratic burden to bear.

While we are not, of course, unused to bearing bureaucratic burdens, it is a more serious aspect of the question which has generated our consistent opposition.

The creation of such an Assembly must inevitably lead to the identification and pursuit of separate union interests - to Scottish rather than British engineering interested - Scottish plumbers rather than British - back to a Scottish Miners Union rather than the NUM.

The development of a division at a time when, if we are to counterbalance the great and growing economic power of multinational companies, the need is to extend existing unity. In one brief emotional spasm we would have sounded the death knell of half a century's effort and progress towards a much needed unity on a United Kingdom scale. (*Alloa Advertiser*, 9th February 1979: 4).

Local Yes and No Campaign Groups

The *Scotland Says No* Stirling Support Group was established formally on Tuesday 16th January 1979 at a public meeting in the Golden Lion hotel in Stirling, with Lord Wilson of Langside as the main speaker (*Stirling Observer*, 10th January 1979: 2): meaning that the chairman of SSN was involved in launching the group locally in the town. Wilson's speech was reported in the next edition of the *Stirling Observer*, where he sought to emphasise that the real question in the referendum was whether an assembly would 'promote better government in Scotland.' (*Stirling Observer*, 17th January 1979: 3). Scotland Says No also funded an advert in the *Stirling Observer* on 14th February 1979 (p.8). The advert was headlined – 'Warning. This Referendum is dangerous.' This advert was repeated in the *Stirling Observer* on 23rd February, with a quarter page advert on page 12. Adverts also appeared in the *Alloa Advertiser* stating that an Assembly means 'more taxes, more government, more bureaucracy, more conflict, less power in Westminster and the start of the break-up of Britain' (*Alloa Advertiser*, 2nd February 1979: 12).

The No campaigners were in the relatively easy position of being able to establish a united front. The Yes campaign was quite different, with separate campaigns organised by the SNP, Labour and the Trade Unions and sometimes very real problems in launching any campaign at all. Joint campaigning between the different sides on the Yes campaign was limited to non-existent for very clear political reasons. As Labour campaigner and later MP, Michael Connarty, explained:

> Collaboration, here? Oh my goodness no. Remember I had set out to take a seat off an SNP councillor in '77 and win the council off them in 1980. No it was a war zone, it just was, it was not a place where there was a great deal of scope for working together (SPA/145).

What occurred instead was the SNP and parts of Labour campaigning for a Yes vote in different parts of central Scotland. There was little Labour Yes campaigning in Falkirk besides the local MP Harry Ewing, with a not dissimilar picture on Stirlingshire West as indicated by Dennis Canavan above. In Clackmannan, Labour decided not to campaign on the referendum at all. The party's Westminster candidate, Martin O'Neill, was to campaign in favour of Labour policy along with some other local activists but there was no Labour Yes or No campaign in the area in 1979. It was left to Clackmannan Trades Council to try to construct a Yes campaign in the months leading up to 1st May (*Alloa Advertiser*, 26th January 1979: 5). By contrast, a Yes for Scotland support committee was established in the Hillfoots towns to promote the Yes campaign in the area, where SNP support was stronger (*Alloa Advertiser*, 7th February 1979: 1).

Public meetings were one key mechanism for both sides of the referendum campaign in 1979 – reflecting upon an older style of campaigning compared to now – and an indication of what was actually going on locally in terms of referendum campaigning. Some of these meetings were debates on the devolution issue, whilst others were one-sided affairs by the various campaign groups. For example, Dennis Canavan and Alex Fletcher (Conservative MP for Edinburgh North) spoke on opposite sides of the public debate 'Scottish Assembly Referendum: Yes or No', in the village hall in Killearn on 23rd February 1979 (*Stirling Observer*, 21st February 1979: 2). Canavan was very active in speaking at a series of public meetings titled 'The Labour Party Says Yes to a Scottish Assembly', with meetings in Denny, Stirling University MacRobert Centre, Bridge of Allan, the Tolbooth in Stirling as well as Bannockburn Miner's Welfare club in the last few days before the referendum – sometimes appearing at several meetings a night (*Stirling Observer*, 21st February 1979: 2; *Falkirk Herald*, 24th February 1979: 2). Some of these were aimed directly at Labour supporters – promoted with the slogan Vote Labour-Vote Yes - on the assumption that if Labour voters supported the Yes side then the referendum would be won.

A joint STUC-Labour campaign for a Yes vote held meetings in Larbert, Falkirk and Bo'ness (*Falkirk Herald*, 17th February 1979: 2). The Labour Movement Yes campaign held a public meeting on 27th February in the Tolbooth in Stirling, which featured local MPs Harry Ewing and Dennis Canavan in addition to Alex Kitson representing the Transport and General Works Union and the STUC. Labour Yes supporters also funded Yes campaign adverts in the local press – explicitly making the link between Labour, trade unions, the Co-operative Party and support for the Yes campaign (*Falkirk Herald*, 24th February 1979: 10). Labour Yes supporters also organised a Yes campaign event on 26th February in Alloa, featuring NUM Vice-Chair and Communist Mick McGahey, John Smith MP (the devolution Minister) and local Labour candidate Martin O'Neill (*Alloa Advertiser*, 16th February 1979: 7). Alva and Menstrie Labour Party also organised a meeting with Martin O'Neill and the Lord Advocate, Ronald Murray, in support of the Yes campaign on 27th February (*Alloa Advertiser*, 23rd February 1979: 2).

The SNP were also active with a large number of public meetings on the Scottish Assembly during the referendum campaign. Gordon Wilson MP (SNP spokesman on devolution) held a Yes campaign public meeting on Thursday 15th February in the Cowane Centre in Stirling (*Stirling Observer*, 14th February 1979. 2). SNP local branch meetings discussed the referendum issue on several occasions and the party was involved in promoting devolution at a public meeting in Dunblane on 26th February, that featured the SNP candidate for Kinross and West Perthshire Iain Smith, Professor Robert Silver, Lord Perth (a former Conservative government Minister under McMillan), Rev. Donald Shaw and Jimmy Nairn (*Stirling Observer*, 21st February

1979: 2). Stirling SNP sought to organise voter surveys to sample local attitudes to devolution ahead of the referendum, knowing that the local party faced multiple electoral contests in the shape of the referendum, likely UK general election and first European election in June 1979 (Stirling SNP Branch, 1978). George Reid was active with meetings along the Hillfoots towns of Alva, Tillicoultry and Dollar (SPA/171), as well as Clackmannan, Strathdevon, Tullibody and Menstrie as part of a campaign of 25 campaign meetings in the lead up to the referendum (*Alloa Advertiser*, 31ˢᵗ January 1979: 2). Reid's campaign meetings also stretched to areas outside his own constituency such as Airth, Carronshore, Skinflats, Polmont and Maddiston in February (*Falkirk Herald*, 3ʳᵈ February 1979: 3). This approach continued with meetings late in February in Whitecross, Shieldhill, Slammanan and Avonbridge (*Falkirk Herald*, 17ᵗʰ February 1979: 3). The party also discussed the referendum issue and campaign at various party meetings in Stirling (*Stirling Observer*, 17ᵗʰ January 1979: 7), Bridge of Allan (*Stirling Observer*, 31ˢᵗ January 1979) and Bannockburn (*Stirling Observer*, 14ᵗʰ February 1979: 5).

Scotland Says No was quick to organise in Stirling, with its inaugural campaign meeting in the Golden Lion hotel on 16ᵗʰ January. Scotland Says No sought to set up a campaign organisation in Falkirk (*Falkirk Herald*, 2ⁿᵈ February 1979: 2), though Labour locally was actually active as the unofficial No campaign. Scotland Says No held a public meeting in Dunblane on 21ˢᵗ February with Teddy Taylor and Rev Andrew Herron as the main speakers followed by a second meeting on 28ᵗʰ February in the Albert Halls in Stirling, with Conservative MP and Shadow Secretary of State for Scotland, Teddy Taylor, as well as Alan Hutton and Lord Wilson of Langside (*Stirling Observer*, 21ˢᵗ February 1979: 2). SSN also held a meeting in the Crown Hotel in Kippen, that featured Tom Begg from the Conservatives and Ronald Burns from Labour (*Stirling Observer*, 28ᵗʰ February 1979: 2). Meetings may have been a relatively small feature of the SSN campaign, but the group had funds for a range of No adverts in the local newspapers during the campaign (*Stirling Observer*, 14ᵗʰ February 1979: 8; 21ˢᵗ February 1979: 12; *Alloa Advertiser*, 2ⁿᵈ February 1979: 12; 7ᵗʰ February 1979: 12) and sought to advance their cause through press releases from local

81

Conservative associations via Westminster parliamentary candidates in the area which set out the case against a Scottish Assembly (*Falkirk Herald*, 17th February 1979: 12) as well as writing letters to the press (*Falkirk Herald*, 24th February 1979: 14). In Clackmannanshire, the Conservatives were active in the No campaign and aimed to distribute 10,000 leaflets in addition to holding a series of public meetings (*Alloa Advertiser*, 19th January 1979: 3), as well as holding local party meetings to promote the No campaign (*Alloa Advertiser*, 23rd February 1979: 2). Besides his extensive letter writing campaign (discussed in chapter 3), Tam Dalyell also spoke on behalf of the No campaign in Larbert at a meeting of Stirlingshire and Clackmannan Labour Party (*Falkirk Herald*, 10th February 1979: 13) and at Central Scotland Chamber of Commerce in Polmont during the campaign (*Falkirk Herald*, 24th February 1979: 13)

The Referendum Result and Outcome

The counting areas for the 1979 devolution referendum were the 9 former regional councils and the 3 islands authorities. This makes for limited but not inaccurate comparisons with the subsequent referendums of 1997 and 2014. Turnout in 1979 was 63.8 per cent and, the turnout combined with the balance of the Yes-No voting had a decisive impact on the result through the operation of the 40 per cent rule that had been inserted into the Scotland Act 1978. Locally, Clackmannanshire, Falkirk and Stirling were all subsumed within Central Region Council. Turnout in the area was a respectable 66.7 per cent with Yes winning 71,296 votes (54.7 per cent) to 59,105 No votes (45.3 per cent): which was the second highest Yes vote after the Western Isles. However, when the 40 per cent rule was applied, Central only had an effective Yes vote of 36.4 per cent. This was repeated across Scotland, where there was a balance of Yes voting regions like Fife, Highland, Lothian and Strathclyde, but also No voting regions like Borders, Dumfries and Galloway, Grampian and Tayside. Amongst the islands, the Western Isles delivered the strongest Yes vote at 55.8 per cent, whilst Orkney and Shetland were resounding No areas (Yes won 27.9 per cent and 27.1 per cent respectively). Overall, the Yes vote in Scotland stood at 1,230,937 (51.6 per cent) to 1,153,502 votes for No (48.4 per cent): and when the 40 per cent rule was applied, it was clear that only 32.9 per cent had voted in support of a Scottish Assembly. Devolution was now politically dead for a time.

Conclusion

The 1979 devolution referendum offers an interesting example of a referendum forced onto a government by its own internal and external opponents. Opponents not only created the referendum device, but also insisted it contained a special majority arrangement – the 40 per cent rule – that was to prove fatal to the prospects of a Scottish Assembly at the time. The 40 per cent rule was controversial and has not been repeated. Even one of its key proponents has had second thoughts about its impact. Writing in this autobiography in 2011, Tam Dalyell reflected that:

> With the benefit of hindsight.......I have come to believe that imposing a 40% hurdle was a mistake. People in Scotland had been used to abiding by simple majorities. Unfortunately, from my point of view, but alas, understandably, the 40% condition was seen as 'not quite right' and 'downright cheating' by others. Undoubtedly it cost the 'no' campaign votes. How many votes, none of us will ever know. But, in my opinion, it was enough to have given the 'no' campaign outright victory in the popular vote....Had there been an outright 'no', the issue of a Scottish Assembly might have been put to bed for a generation (Dalyell 2011: 185).

The 40 per cent rule was important. But so were the economic and political conditions – which were very far from what we would regard as 'winning conditions' for a referendum, with economic chaos, recession and political instability within the Labour Government. The divisions within Labour over devolution were very real and existed at all levels of the party. Linked to its tribal disputes with the SNP, it made for a very fragmented campaign in Scotland, with

Labour campaigning both Yes and No in 1979 as well as not at all in some places. Disunity was a key factor and this fed through to voters who received very mixed messages if any from the governing party that was electorally and institutionally dominant in many parts of Scotland. Having said all that, a campaign of sorts, was attempted. It had some *ad hoc* qualities nationally and locally and was heavily conditioned by party divisions and lack of commitment and enthusiasm on the ground. It was a traditional campaign of leafleting, canvassing and some polling day work but does not seem to have been very convincing or of high intensity.

Three further party political points are worth reflecting upon. First, the referendum experience produced huge internal conflict within the SNP that effectively disabled the party as an electoral force until the mid-1980s. The SNP was one of the main victims of devolution, the referendum and 5 years of constitutional debate. Second, the experience not only increased the level of hostility and tribalism between Labour and the SNP but it caused huge difficulties for any cross-party work or consensus on constitutional change. This problem ran through the 1980s, with mutual suspicions towards initiatives like the campaign for a Scottish Assembly and the Scottish Constitutional Convention. Third, over time, the Conservatives also suffered from the 1979 referendum experience. Although the party had emerged in a strong position from the referendum – the Scottish assembly was not created, it had avoided internal splits and gone on to win the 1979 general election – its role at the referendum and position in Scotland was set for a significant decline and then a complete collapse (Mitchell 1990).

Endnotes

1.   System 3 opinion poll, Gerry Hassan and Peter Lynch (2001), *The Almanac of Scottish Politics*, London: Politicos, p.379.
2.   Opinion poll data taken from collated data on opinion poll support for the main British parties from 1974-1979 at ukpollingreport.co.uk.
3.   Opinion polls by System 3, contained in Gerry Hassan and Peter Lynch (2011), *The Almanac of Scottish Politics*, pp.379-380.

4.   Unemployment statistics from Office of National statistics - https://www.ons.gov.uk/employmentandlabourmarket/peoplenotinwork/unemployment/timeseries/mgsx

5.   Office of National Statistics time series data at the National Archives http://webarchive.nationalarchives.gov.uk

6.   Bank of England data at http://www.bankofengland.co.uk/statistics.

7.   Stewart Stevenson, then chairman of West Lothian SNP constituency association, in David Torrance (2010), *Salmond: Against the Odds*, Birlinn, p.55. And, the Alex he is talking about is Alex Salmond.

4

The 1997 Devolution Referendum

Introduction

In a sense, the road to the 1997 devolution referendum started at the failed referendum of 1979. It's worth remembering that the narrow result had actually been a small victory for Yes, which was undone by the 40 per cent rule. Supporters of devolution were disillusioned after the 1979 referendum experience and it was a formative experience for many who would be involved in politics for years to come, especially in relation to attitudes and behaviours between Labour and the SNP. However, campaigners did not give up on the issue of constitutional change, despite the divisive nature of the referendum and its effect on cross-party relations in Scotland. Indeed, one of the many challenges for campaigners post-1979 was to get Labour and the SNP to debate constitutional change within their own parties without it turning into an exercise that would turn devolutionists against centralists and gradualists against fundamentalists or an opportunity to bash the other party. To some extent, both parties turned inwards after 1979, to disputes over ideology, positioning and the constitution, with evident bitterness about the referendum experience and how to move politics forward in the early 1980s. Second, the Home Rule campaigners had to promote dialogue that could generate a broad consensus on change that also involved a detailed set of proposals for devolution itself – gaining party support for that would be difficult, not least as inter-party contestation on devolution/nationalism became a renewed feature of Labour-SNP competition throughout these years Finally, Home Rulers had to campaign for a devolved institution themselves amongst the public and hope that party politics did not wreck their efforts. Of course, during these years, the issue of a referendum was not the objective of supporters of change - rather they sought to generate an elite and popular consensus for a scheme of Home Rule that would gain maximum support. When the two-question referendum proposal came along in 1996, it was controversial and viewed with some suspicion, not least given concerns over Labour's commitment to devolution under Tony Blair.[1]

The 1997 devolution referendum was not merely a product of Labour's electoral victory at the general election and the party's more secure position on devolution across the UK. It was also the consequence of a long and varied period of social movement mobilisation by proponents of constitutional change from across the political parties and from none that began after the 1979 referendum. Indeed, one argument that will be put forward here is that there was a large amount of Yes campaigning before the referendum itself, with a range of different initiatives by parties, pressure groups and trade unions, long before the referendum occurred. Therefore, whilst this chapter focuses on the limited period of the 1997 referendum campaign, there were several campaigns before it that helped to build support for a Yes vote over the longer term. This began very early, with the creation of the Campaign for a Scottish Assembly in 1979, with its formal launch on 1st March 1980 – a year after the failed referendum (McLean 2005: 47). The CSA sought to be a cross-party organization that aimed at creating a constitutional convention as a representative body to design a Scottish Assembly. The intention here was to get a host of political organisations to contribute to an Assembly, to give it popular form, support and legitimacy. It led in time to the Constitutional Steering Committee, Claim of Right and Scottish Constitutional Convention of 1989-1995. This mobilisation process also involved a wide range of initiatives, often involving the Scottish Trades Union Congress and its component trade unions – who had played key roles in the 1979 referendum campaign and continued to do so afterwards. Organisations such as the Campaign for a Scottish Assembly (later the Campaign for a Scottish Parliament), the Radical Scotland collective (a populariser of the Doomsday scenario idea before the 1987 general election), the Destiny Marchers, Democracy for Scotland, Common Cause, Scotland United, Scottish Labour Action, etc., all played a role in generating interest and support for constitutional change within the political parties (especially within Labour) and within institutions like local government. So, multiple initiatives sought to maintain support for change, using a variety of different strategies and organisations to advance their cause (Mitchell 1996) and, in short, the Yes campaign kept developing.

Two significant factors also made the 1997 Scottish referendum experience different from that of 1979: timing and the nature of the referendum question. First of all, this time around Labour controlled the referendum process. Whereas the 1979 referendum had been forced on a minority Labour government late in its term of office, this time around the intention was to hold the referendum early in the honeymoon period of the New Labour government to give the issue momentum and protect Labour's position at the 1997 UK general election – if it was able to demonstrate a clear commitment to early implementation of devolution, it would ensure it didn't leak votes to the SNP that could undermine its electoral prospects in 1997. Momentum would also protect Labour from internal opposition to devolution, which was such a feature of the 1979 experience. As the former Labour MP and anti-devolutionist Brian Wilson pointed out 'Donald (Dewar) never forgot that and that is why when the opportunity arose again in 1997 there was no delay and no time for any dissidence in Labour to arise that would have done if he had waited another six months' (SPA/763). Labour's overwhelming electoral success in 1997, firm leadership and the rapid implementation of the referendum all had a role in maintaining Labour as well as cross-party unity around the campaign.

The second significant change involved the wording and format of the referendum question, which were very controversial when introduced. This referendum featured two questions – one on support for a Scottish Parliament, one on support for the parliament to have tax-varying powers. This latter question had its origins in two developments. The issue of tax powers had been a recurrent theme in the debates around devolution for several decades – and remains so today. After discussing various potential tax schemes, the Scottish Constitutional Convention settled upon proposing that the Scottish

Parliament would have the power to vary the lower rate of income tax by +/-3p (Scottish Constitutional Convention 1995). In terms of tax and spending powers, this was not a significant tax power. However, it was symbolically important in political terms for both sides of the devolution debate – for opponents it served to confirm that devolution would involve tax rises, for supporters it served as an example that devolution would involve some rather than no taxation powers: meaning that devolution in 1997 was stronger than in 1979. However, political experience meant that Labour viewed the tax issue with caution. Income tax had been a highly sensitive topic in UK politics for some time, to the extent that Labour leader Tony Blair ruled out any rise in income tax if elected into government at the 1997 general election. Earlier in the 1990s, Scottish Labour's proposals to replace the poll tax (community charge) with a new system of local government funding had been dubbed a 'roof tax' by the Conservatives. The Conservatives set about depicting the devolved income tax power as a 'tartan tax', so Labour was aware that the tax question needed careful handing. The solution was the two question referendum format, which allowed voters to support devolution without having to commit to the tax arrangements. It had the effect of placing a protective cordon around the devolved parliament and also had the effect of directing the No campaign to focus on the tax issue.

The Political and Economic Context

The political context for devolution at the 1997 referendum was generally positive and certainly much more positive than in 1979. The UK general election of 1997 created favourable conditions for the referendum in a number of ways. First, and most obviously, Labour had triumphed at the general election. The party not only won the election but it won by a landslide. Its UK support increased to 43.2 per cent (+8.8 per cent) and it finished the election with 418 seats and a majority of 179. This majority was especially useful as it would cushion the party from dissent by its own MPs during the devolution debates in the House of Commons and also prove effective in reversing any changes to devolution proposals by the House of Lords: in short, the exact opposite of the experience at Westminster in the 1974-9, when Labour devo-sceptics changed the content of the Scotland and Wales Acts against the wishes of a minority Labour government. Second, in Scotland, Labour won 45.6 per cent in 1997 and increased its number of seats to 56. Meantime, Conservative support declined to 17.5 per cent and the party lost all of its 11 MPs – effecting its capacity to oppose devolution at all levels. When you add in the SNP on 22.1 per cent and 6 seats and the Liberal Democrats on 13 per cent and 10 seats, you see the pro-constitutional changes parties had all of the seats and 80.7 per cent of the vote. And, this situation continued up to referendum day itself. Of course, it's worth remembering that the combined electoral support of the pro-change parties in 1979 was 75 per cent between Labour, the SNP and the Liberals but it did not deliver success on that scale by any means.

After the decisive general election result, support for Labour remained strong and the party's popularity plus the honeymoon effect enjoyed by the new Blair government assisted in creating 'winning conditions' for a Yes Yes vote in September. Opinion polls by System 3 found support for Labour in Scotland increased to 57 per cent after the general election and remained at 50 per cent and above until September. Indeed, the party was polling 55 per cent in September 1997. Support for the SNP and Liberal Democrats also remained relatively constant from the general election to the referendum, with some slight slippage by the Liberal Democrats to 9 per cent in September. However, it was the position of the Conservatives that had changed most. The general election had been catastrophic at all levels in Britain, but in Scotland the party had lost all of its seats and seen its vote fall to 17.5 per cent. System 3 saw no recovery in support after the election so that the Conservatives stood at 13 per cent in September (Hassan and Lynch 2001: 385). The only electoral test that fell within the period of the referendum campaign was the Paisley North by-election of 6th November 1997. This potentially hazardous by-election occurred as a result of the suicide of the sitting MP, Gordon McMaster, on 28th July, accompanied by accusations of bullying by another Labour MP. The by-election was difficult as it involved a key, long-term Labour-SNP battleground constituency with the potential to destabilize the new-found referendum unity of the main Yes parties and damage the referendum campaign. In the event, the by-election conflict did not leak into the referendum and Labour held the seat with 44.1 per cent of the vote to SNP's 32.5 per cent as the by-election's timing helped to create a distance from the referendum campaign.

In the months between the UK general election of May 1997 and the referendum itself, support for devolution remained strong in opinion polls, though with clear differences in the nature of support for a Scottish Parliament and one with tax-varying powers. Polls on the parliament showed support comfortably above 60 per cent, with System 3 recording 68 per cent in July 1997 and MORI showing 67 per cent on 8th September (Denver et al 2000: 123). Opposition to the parliament was recorded in the range between 21 and 25 per cent during this period, with the Don't Knows moving between 10-19 per cent (Denver et al 2000: 123). Both System 3 and ICM polled voters on the issue of support for the parliament on the eve of the referendum on 10th September. System 3 found Yes on 61 per cent, No on 20 per cent and Don't Knows at 19 per cent. ICM found Yes was higher at 63 per cent, No on 25 per cent and a smaller number of Don't Knows on 12 per cent (Denver 2000: 123). The final result recorded a total of 74.3 per cent to 25.7 per cent in favour of the parliament. The issue of tax-varying powers showed much narrower levels of support in opinion polls, with support for tax powers in a range between 45 and 56 per cent, compared to opposition moving between 26 and 38 per cent, whilst the Don't Knows moved between 15 and 24 per cent (Denver et al 2000: 124). The opinion poll by System 3 on the 10th September – the day before the referendum itself – recorded Yes on 45 per cent, No on 31 per cent and Don't Knows on 24 per cent (Denver 2000: 124). Though the final result saw Yes on 63.5 per cent to 36.5 per cent for No. And, given the patterns of these polls, devolution had a strong headwind behind it in the months leading up to the referendum. As a consequence, both the national and local campaigns focused less on conversion or persuasion than on turning out devolution supporters and voters of pro-change parties to ensure that the pro-devolution majority voted.

The economic context in 1997 was relatively benign, though conditioned by careful Labour positioning on taxation at both the Scottish and UK levels. The Labour Party fought the 1997 general election on economic competence, having spent years trying to establish economic credibility in the City of London and in the country in general. In the years leading up to the referendum, it was the Conservatives that were responsible for the economy and economic performance – as they had been since 1979. During this period, interest rates were still determined by the UK Government - not independently by the Bank of England as was to follow after the 1997 general election – and moved in a narrow band from averages of 6.5 per cent in 1995, down to 5.8 per cent in 1996 and then up again to 6.5 per cent in 1997.[2] Inflation was modest with averages of 3.5 per cent in 1995, 2.4 per cent in 1996 and then 3.1 per cent in 1997.[3] Finally, UK unemployment was 8.3 per cent at the end 1995, falling to 7.8 per cent at the end of 1996 and 6.7 per cent in September 1997 when the referendum was held.[4] Scottish unemployment lagged behind this figure, falling from 8.7 per cent in 1995 down to 8.6 per cent in 1997 (Scottish Government 2007).

The National Campaign

The national campaign efforts in 1997 were much more straightforward than in 1979. There were only two umbrella campaign groups – Scotland Forward and Think Twice – though the political parties and trades unions were also important, not least in publicizing the issues around devolution and mobilizing voter support in the days and weeks leading up to the vote on 11th September 1997. Scotland Forward managed to establish something like 20 local groups, with local campaign coordinators, but Think Twice had no local organization and relied upon local Conservative associations to deliver its campaign on the ground. There was also much greater harmony between the parties about campaign cooperation and avoiding unnecessary conflict that would undermine support for devolution. The organizational patterning of the two campaigns was also different from 1979. This time around, it was Yes who had the foresight to know a referendum was coming and planning began in 1996 with meetings, the commissioning of research and early thinking about what the campaign would look like (Denver et al 2000: 52). Yes also had the negative template of 1979 to influence their activities as well as the cross-party cooperation of the Scottish Constitutional Convention. The Convention had produced a compromise plan for a Scottish Parliament and it had also helped to create productive relationships between Labour and the Liberal Democrats. The No campaign did not organize until after the May 1997 general election and, even then, was slow to be established and begin operations. It never really caught up.

Whilst umbrella groups were established at the referendum, the political parties remained integral. Scotland Forward certainly developed as a structure with local campaigners outwith party politics willing to undertake campaigning through local branches and groups with its own material, but the parties themselves and their national and local organizations were central as we shall see – they knew where their supporters were and sought to contact them at the referendum. Often, it was the local party constituency organization, branch or offices that were the basis of the campaign. Whilst there was no electoral threshold as there had been in 1979 – no 40 per cent rule – there was an awareness that a low turnout amongst Yes Yes supporters could undermine the legitimacy of the referendum result and also cause some difficulties on the second question on tax-varying powers for the Scottish Parliament. Ensuring that the potential Yes Yes majority actually turned out on referendum day was a preoccupation of Yes campaigners, reflected in uneasiness at the suspension of campaigning for a week following the death of Princess Diana in Paris: would it involve a loss of political momentum that demobilized supporters of change?

On the Yes side, avoiding a replay of the inter-party hostilities of 1979 was seen as a key part of the campaign, especially as conflict between Labour and the SNP remained strong as a consequence of the 1997 election contest. Scotland Forward chair Nigel Smith was determined to avoid the continuing enmity between Labour and the SNP due to a renewed period of constitutional and policy competition in the 1990s – fearing it would undermine the campaign and fail to deliver a Yes vote. Smith had a number of conversations with the Scottish Constitutional Convention and with the SNP to try to create a cross-party campaign in 1996. He also held strategy discussions in early 1997 with the Scottish

Constitutional Convention and with Labour. He attemped to secure funding and prepare for the referendum well before the 1997 general election, with the supportive involvement of the STUC. Despite the early start, Scotland Forward suffered from a lack of funds throughout the referendum period and was £20,000 in the red at the end of the campaign due to office, staff and materials costs. Whilst Scotland Forward produced a unified campaign, it did not produce an integrated campaign – that was seen to be impossible due to the different attitudes and interests of the political parties. Labour was keen to build on its general election success by running its own campaign and didn't want its logo on the Scotland Forward leaflet. However, a compromise was reached to use party colours on leaflets rather than logos, so there was some integration of party and Yes branding. For Nigel Smith, a successful campaign settled around one specific goal:

> The only strategic aim of the campaign was to prevent an outbreak of argument about policy or person between the SNP and Labour. But it was nothing I could make a song and dance about. And I didn't. I talked about a unifying campaign and talked about Scotland Forward, all the positives involved. People have great difficulty in thinking that a strategy can have such a negative base. But that, I promise you was all that mattered to me. If we had an outbreak of arguing, either about independence or about people as individuals, basically the Scots would stay at home, they would not vote No but they would stay at home and we would not get the decisive result that we needed. So the whole strategy rested on two ideas. One was that there was already – that the Scots had already settled that there had to be a change. And secondly the only thing that would prevent us getting there was an outbreak of argument between the two principal parties and that was the strategy (SPA/753/1).

Other political actors shared the importance of preventing inter-party and personality conflicts. Liberal Democrat MP Menzies Campbell echoed Smith's view and stated that

> There was a huge determination that there should not be the kind of splits there were before. And if there were people who were not keen

94

on appearing on platforms with other people then they kept their mouths shut about it and didn't appear (SPA/766).

Conflict prevention and managing the different parties was a central part of the campaign for Scotland Forward. But, it also had two other roles. It had to coordinate and undertake actual campaigning and ensure the political parties delivered on the ground, but also act to provide a mechanism for cooperation for the national and local campaign effort. Scottish Labour general secretary Jack McConnell explained the need for coordination to ensure that the grassroots levels of the political parties actually functioned at the referendum:

> We were also always aware that when it came down to individual campaigners on the streets delivering leaflets and putting up posters, you know doing the town centre work on a Saturday morning, without the three parties doing that, that would not happen on the scale that it was required. So behind the scenes of Scotland Forward the three party Chief Execs and our key organisers and our key PR people were meeting very regularly because we realised that we had to deliver the goods here. You could get the tone and the presentation and the engagement in the campaign right. But ultimately if you did not have the troops on the ground doing the campaigning you were not going to win (SPA/790).

Labour was certainly not inactive at the referendum. The party's strategy and messaging was guided by a series of focus groups during the short referendum campaign to test awareness of the referendum, the taxation issue, positive and negative attitudes to devolution etc. The party's central organisation produced campaign packs for 8 regional coordinators across Scotland as well as the local coordinators in the CLPs, with a range of Labour Yes Yes leaflets, draft press materials, flags, art work, posters, stickers, etc., with briefings on devolution and key campaign messages (Scottish Labour Party 1997). Some of the leaflets also doubled up as membership recruitment leaflets, as Labour sought to capitalize on its level of popularity at the 1997 general election and help build for future contests. For some, the goal of the campaign was simply about the mobilization of supporters of devolution as a majority in favour of change had been evident in opinion polls for some time. The idea was not to spend time converting voters on the issue of a Scottish Parliament, rather that there was a large but latent majority for change that need to come down to the polling stations to deliver devolution. As Yes campaigner Kevin Dunion argued

> In large part the Scotland Forward grouping was focused on getting the vote out, taking the temperature of the people and doing a – I was going to say bread and butter - but more than that, cake and candy stuff to get people out. It wasn't a highly politicised campaign, I think we were highly confident that if we could get the vote out we would win the referendum (SPA/767).

Such efforts required national and local campaigners undertaking some of the more mundane but important tasks in political campaigns. Esther Robertson explained some of her daily activities for Scotland Forward in its Edinburgh office in Forth Street as

> Coming in from Bathgate with a luggage trolley, parcelling stuff up and hiking it up to the bus station and putting it on buses for Inverness and Fort William and all of that... it was all hand knitted and informal, but there was no shortage of enthusiasm and willingness (SPA/776).

On the other side of the referendum campaign, Think Twice faced different problems. On the one hand, though it entered the campaign relatively late, it did manage to raise funds for its activities and ended up marginally outspending Scotland Forward by £275,000 to £270,000 (Denver et al 2000: 59). Some of the money came in small donations, some in large amounts. However, the campaign lacked strategy and planning due to its late start. The organization tended to get bogged down in day to day activities rather than planning and executing overall strategy. For example, campaign chief Peter Fraser pointed out that

> Bluntly it was pretty embryonic in form. And the idea that we had a network round the country just simply wasn't true. We did not have time to do that. It was really only in the last few days of the

referendum that we started building up anything like a head of steam. I can remember we had a very large committee meeting with some really quite influential people, which is now a hotel in Glasgow in Blythswood Square, but it was then the Royal Automobile Club. And we had a meeting and that was the first time it was gelling. If that meeting had taken place six weeks beforehand that was what we really needed so that we could set out a blueprint for what we wanted to do in Scotland (SPA/791).

According to Fraser, even with improving organization, some relatively simple things failed for lack of planning:

By the time we decided we could do a mail drop in every household in Scotland the only date that the Post Office could give us was a week after the referendum in Scotland (SPA/791).

When it came to trying to gain public support from celebrities to oppose devolution, Think Twice also faced problems due to people becoming much more supportive of devolution and also, not being prepared to take a position of public opposition on the issues. As Peter Fraser stated:

We tried a number of people, prominent sportsmen and things like that. We were really quite shocked to discover that when we got to the list that they were saying things like 'No we are not going to add our names, we actually think this is a good idea.' And we had a number of people who were strongly against it but did not want to have their names associated with a political campaign (SPA/791).

Of course, behind organizational and strategic questions about the effectiveness of Think Twice there were some fairly solid and negative political realities militating against the efforts of the No campaign. Former Liberal Democrat MP Menzies Campbell described the 1997 referendum as a huge political challenge for opponents of devolution that was difficult to surmount:

It was a kind of reversal of 1979. The No campaign was not particularly successful. It never really got off the ground and it was associated with Thatcher, although Thatcher had long since gone, six or seven years – longer, nearly ten years before. Nonetheless the forces of opposition to devolution were certainly associated with the Thatcher, then Major era. The whole country Scotland, England, Northern Ireland and Wales had comprehensively booted out the Tory Government. So to be associated with that strand of the political agenda was very damaging to the No campaign and it never really got off the ground (SPA/766).

The Local Campaign

Whilst a good deal of the national campaign sought to avoid the mistakes of 1979 – with divided campaign groups and damaging tribal divisions between Labour and the SNP – avoiding such repetitions was also important on the ground at the level of local campaigning: especially as those rivalries could be highly personal and also long-standing. The three Yes parties agreed that where a party had the local MP, they would take a lead in campaigning and that would work for local council wards too (Denver et al 2000: 104). The intention was to mitigate the potential for local turf wars and encourage as much Yes campaigning as possible by local parties. Of course, in terms of timing and political environment, the 1997 experience was different. Whereas the 1979 referendum was influenced by the imminent UK general election, with partisan considerations focused on that rather than devolution, 1997 had seen the general election deliver a Labour landslide, with no immediate and linked electoral event to follow (the 1999 Scottish election was to be some time away and that helped). In short, the devolution referendum was to appear quickly after the general election and appear as a sole campaign event: unlike the 1979 and 2014 experiences.

Moreover, just as the political landscape had altered nationally, with Labour dominance and Conservative decline after 18 years in power, the local picture had changed markedly too. The Conservatives lost all 11 seats in Scotland in 1997, by huge amounts of votes. The consequence was to reduce institutional opposition to devolution via elected politicians but also take the steam and activism out of local

No campaigns. The rapid timetable for the referendum also prevented the emergence of an organised anti-devolution opposition from the Conservatives or from Labour devo-sceptics either. Moreover, Labour had extended its electoral reach into new urban, rural and suburban areas - Inverness, Strathkelvin and Bearsden, Dumfries for example – and also won Stirling handsomely from the Conservatives. The new Labour MP, Anne McGuire, won 47.8 per cent of the vote and turned a former Conservative-Labour marginal into a safe seat (until 2015 when the SNP won Stirling). The Conservative vote declined to 32.5 per cent and the prominent MP and Secretary of State for Scotland, Michael Forsyth, left active politics after the election and took a finance job in London. In nearby Ochil constituency (known as Clackmannan at other times), Labour won with 45 per cent of the vote, whilst the SNP polled a strong second with 34.4 per cent through fielding the former MP George Reid. Finally, in the two Falkirk seats, East and West, the Labour candidate won with 56.1 per cent and 59.3 per cent, with the SNP putting in strong second places finishes in each seat. The end result locally, was a much stronger political environment in favour of constitutional change, with substantial Labour and SNP votes and serious Conservative decline. Losing the only MP in the area and the damaging effect on morale and organization of the 1997 wipeout also structured the environment in favour of change and away from the No campaign. The local balance shifted towards change and the elected MPs all played a role in campaigning for a Yes Yes vote at the devolution referendum in September, against a diminished No campaign.

So, how did the referendum campaign work out on the ground? Well, the surveys on the local campaign by Denver et al (2000) discovered that there were positive attitudes to coordinating campaigning with other parties and with Scotland Forward and most local organisations campaigned at the referendum (Denver et al 2000: 105-6). However, the type of campaigning was different and of a different intensity. Leaflet distribution was the key function, but there was a strong degree of local organization compared to 1979, especially within local Labour parties, which all had local organisers at the referendum (Denver et al 2000: 108). There were few public meetings held compared to 1979, but more of a focus on doorstep canvassing, telephone canvassing and knocking up on referendum day to ensure supporters turned out (Denver et al 2000: 110). When it came to campaign intensity, most local parties felt the referendum campaign was less intense than at a general election – and they had just fought one in May 1997 – and more like a local election though, one at which Labour were highly active and recorded the strongest activity levels amongst the parties at the referendum (Denver et al 2000: 112-113): a real reversal on the party's level of activity in 1979 and evident at all levels of the party from national officials to MPs and local activists as can be seen from the interviews in this chapter compared with 1979. Moreover, a fair degree of the local campaigning efforts were noticed by the voters before the referendum itself (Denver et al 2000: 118).

Several patterns of campaigning were evident in the local area in 1997 – patterns which worked to the benefit of the Yes Yes campaigners due to better organization as well as very changed political circumstances compared to 1979. Labour in particular, were much more united behind devolution and also more coordinated in their activities locally as Denver et al's surveys demonstrated above, particularly to utilize the local press to promote devolution. Labour had opened a campaign office in Stirling with a full-time staff member several years before the 1997 general election as part of its strategy to win the seat from the Conservatives. The office had been central to the election campaign, through organization, coordination, data collection, etc. and remained active as a campaign hub at the devolution referendum by organizing leafleting, canvassing in areas of support as well as polling day duty. The office gave Labour a clear organizational advantage to its campaign through its data collection, accompanied by a newly elected MP.

Local Scotland Forward coordinator Doug Maugham offered some insight into local campaigning in Stirling generally, though most obviously the Yes campaign. He was a Labour Party member (later a candidate) who sought to generate local activity in support of the Yes vote:

> Locally, it was a bit of a mix. Obviously, it was a joint effort among the Labour Party, the Scottish Nationalists and Lib Dems who all came in for the 'Yes Yes' vote. The Tories were against, and they were campaigning on the other side, but on the 'Yes Yes' side of the

referendum, there was a mixed bag. A lot of it was obviously from the parties, and their local activists and their local reps working together, and then there were other people who, when they heard the campaign was being established locally, came forward through one means or another, and volunteered to work. A lot of people, pretty non-political, hadn't been involved with the party before, but were interested in campaigning for a 'Yes' vote in the referendum (SPA/146).

Some of the local activity was divided between the political parties, as we shall see below, whilst some was carried out by small groups of Scotland Forward activists. Some of the public activity involved campaigning in prominent locations in the area that, in Stirling's case, usually meant in and around the Thistle shopping centre. The Thistle was not only in the centre of Stirling, but large enough to attract shoppers from areas around Stirling too, so it acted as a magnet for campaigners in 1997 and at all types of elections (and at the 2014 referendum). As Doug Maugham pointed out:

> It was largely a question of going to places where, ideally, people would come to us. The idea in Stirling was central Stirling and Port Street, any day of the week but particularly on a Saturday: hundreds and hundreds of people going by, and you've got the chance to set up a stall, which we did, and attract people's attention – you put up some balloons, you give some balloons to kids, all the rest of that stuff, so it's a question of attracting some attention and then engaging people for a little while until you get your message across, but also to mainly – not just getting the message across individually, but raising awareness that the referendum's coming up, and it's important that you go out and vote (SPA/146).

Besides stalls and public meetings, there was also some doorstep work in terms of leafleting, some soft canvassing and knocking up of voters on referendum day. Often, the campaigning was influenced by the fact that most voters were supportive of a Yes Yes vote and only needed encouragement/reminding to vote, rather than a hard sell on the merits of devolution itself. One of the things campaigners used was pledge cards, which was essentially a pledge to vote Yes at the referendum, which voters would sign, as a way to remind them to support the parliament and turn out to vote. And, for the most part, according to Maugham, it worked:

> I remember it as being a good natured campaign, which certainly political campaigns aren't always. It was done in a good spirit, with the three parties working well together, and there was a good mood about the campaign. There'd been a very positive mood in the lead up to the General Election in '97, and, as you may recall, the mood after the 1st May 1997, and I know things changed in the years to follow, but it certainly, in the early stages of the Labour Government in 1997, there was a very positive political mood generally, and I think that's why, again with hindsight, looking back, it was particularly good that the referendum campaign kicked off as soon as it did, if there'd been a gap of a year, or two years, moods do change, and I think certainly there was still that bit of a wave that we were riding on of interest, and optimism, and enthusiasm - for politics, for the Labour Government, and that carried forward to the referendum campaign as well (SPA/146).

One of the legacies of Labour's increased professionalization ahead of the 1997 general election was improved organisation at the national and local level – meaning full-time staff, campaign offices in places like Stirling and a better degree of coordination of messages and campaigning that were immediately able to be redeployed for the referendum campaign. For example, Stirling's new Labour MP, Anne McGuire, the Ochils MP Martin O'Neill plus mid-Scotland and Fife MEP Alex Falconer coordinated their press statements on devolution in the *Stirling Observer* (*Stirling Observer*, 30th July: 5). The regular MP's column in the paper, which usually involved a report on the MP's work and activities, now focused on promoting devolution. Anne McGuire's column on 30th July discussed the benefits of devolution (*Stirling Observer*, 30th July: 11). McGuire's article was followed up by a similar pro-devolution article on 20th August that was part of a feature on the referendum that also featured former Conservative MP Michael Ancrum, arguing against the referendum. McGuire deployed several arguments in favour of devolution. First, she sought to explain that devolution maintained the Union:

> A Scottish Parliament will serve Stirling, Scotland and the United Kingdom well in years to come. It recognises Scotland's distinctive identity as well as the strong ties that bind us together as one United Kingdom.
> Rather than undermining the union as opponents of a Scottish Parliament claim, devolution will give strength to an enduring partnership.
> This is about DEVOLUTION of power, not separation (*Stirling Observer*, 20th August 1997).

Furthermore, McGuire attempted to put the tax powers into context:

> The tax varying (yes varying, not raising) powers that you will be asked to approve, are just that, powers. When at a later date, you come to vote for parties and individuals to represent you in a Scottish Parliament you will all have the opportunity to see if and how they intend to use those powers (*Stirling Observer*, 20th August 1997).

Michael Ancrum's response for Think Twice picked over some of the same points as well as focusing on cost and bureaucracy, familiar themes from 1979:

> A Scottish Parliament would mean more expensive bureaucracy and more politicians – some 129 more of them at a cost of at least £80,000 per head per year. That's over £10 million spent each and every year on more politicians alone.
> Just think what that kind of money would buy for Scotland's hospitals and schools. Are Scots really prepared to see more of their money being spent on employing another layer of government, all at the expense of our public services? (*Stirling Observer*, 20th August 1997).

This particular issue was linked directly to the proposed taxation powers of the parliament by Ancrum:

> Nowhere are the Government's Scottish parliament plans more faulty and unfair, however, than in their provision for imposing a Tartan Tax – up to 3p in the pound extra income tax on all workers living in Scotland.

The Government claim this to be a 'modest' sum, but I doubt whether many Scottish families would judge a hike of well over £300 in their income tax bills to be modest.

In any event I'm sure most Stirlingshire folk would rather decide for themselves how to spend that kind of money, rather than hand it over to the extra politicians who would sit in a Scottish Parliament in Edinburgh (*Stirling Observer*, 20th August 1997).

However, the fact that Michael Ancrum was the author of the article demonstrated one of Think Twice's problems. Michael Ancrum was a Conservative MP who had lost his seat of Edinburgh South in 1987 but had been elected in Devizes in Wiltshire in 1992: meaning Think Twice was reliant on someone who had not been active in Scottish politics for 10 years. This was a problem Think Twice struggled with throughout the referendum campaign, with their campaign led by Donald Findlay, a Conservative Party officebearer and Vice-Chairman of Rangers Football Club not a full-time party politician (Denver et al 2000: 110). Some of the Yes messages were locally focused, with a pro-devolution article in the *Stirling Observer* written by Labour's Secretary of State for Scotland Donald Dewar just the day before the referendum itself (*Stirling Observer*, 10th September 1997: 6). Even the letters page of the paper was more in favour of devolution, with supportive letters from a local businessman, the Liberal Democrats, etc., along with opposition from the chair of the local Conservative association (*Stirling Observer*, 10th September 1997: 18). Stirling was also a popular place for national campaigns, with both Alastair Darling and William Hague campaigning locally in the week of the referendum to promote each side of the campaign (*Stirling Observer*, 10th September 1997: 6).

For local No campaigners in 1997, the referendum was a challenge, not least due to the general election result and the loss and departure of former Stirling MP Michael Forsyth. The loss of Forsyth created a lack of local leadership at the referendum, in addition to the loss of campaigners after the general election, not least through the decline of Conservative students from Stirling University. In Stirling, the No campaign involved only the local Tories, with limited capacity for campaigning beyond leafleting and some door knocking.[5] The party still had the Stirling Conservative Association office as a campaign base and it became the local No campaign office but lack of campaigners plus the absence of a cross-party effort against devolution undermined the No campaign. The local Think Twice campaigners organised a few public meetings as well as door knocking in their areas of traditional support but didn't venture out beyond them. The local organization distributed Think Twice leaflets and put up posters, but these were centrally-provided with no local content. What Think Twice was able to provide was also contrasted unfavourably with Labour's national campaign of glossy leaflets, newspapers, etc. It was recognised that Labour were fighting a very party political campaign, directed at its own voters and Think Twice couldn't match them. Where Think Twice campaigners did get some traction was with the issue of tax-varying powers on the doorsteps, but then, that was always likely to be the case in Conservative areas. However, the tax issue never really caught fire in the campaign, instead, it tended to get swamped by the overall issue of a parliament, which favoured the Yes campaign.[6]

When it came to the amount of campaigning undertaken at the referendum, it was clearly seen to be much less high intensity than at a general election – especially for activists who had campaigned in highly contested seats like Ochil and Stirling at the 1997 general election. Some of the campaigning was also focused geographically, given the strong local support for Yes and No in areas of Labour and SNP versus Conservative support, so that the parties concentrated leafleting and door knocking in their strong areas. In any case, despite the limited nature of the campaigning, the result in Stirling was to be a clear double Yes vote. The result was observable by campaigners on the day when they could gauge the level of local support in key areas in Stirling, where support had been more evenly distributed between Yes and No in 1979. Support in working class Cornton, for example, showed that the SNP had mobilized its core vote at the referendum, but also that the Labour Party locally had mobilized its own supporters: factors central to achieving a double Yes vote. Overall, the result was a reflection of the fact that the campaign was more organized than in 1979, with more time for planning and implementation and a clearer idea of what the campaign should aim to do.[7] Whilst a cross-party, non-party campaign was evident in 1997, the political parties and their local campaign organisations were also important. For example, local SNP organizer Jim Thomson remembered that:

> I think, certainly locally, we believed that the only way to win it is if we could get to our core vote – because by that time we had got a lot more sophisticated, we did know where our vote was, and we were convinced we could persuade them we didn't need Scotland Forward. That's not to say we were against what they were doing, but we felt that we had sufficient information to gather votes for the cause (SPA/747).

In Falkirk, there was a good deal of local campaigning in favour of devolution, but still some opposition within Labour to change, that had echoes of the 1979 experience. The fact that the two Falkirk seats were strong areas for both Labour and the SNP helped the Yes campaign, with a prominent and long-term pro-devolution MP in Denis Canavan in Falkirk West plus the support of the new Falkirk East MP Michael Connarty. However, there remained local opposition to devolution in Falkirk West within the Labour Party.[8] Local areas like Camelon were still seen to be anti-devolution even in 1997 with a local branch that hadn't helped at the local Falkirk referendum on devolution in December 1993 sponsored by the Scottish Constitutional Convention (Mitchell 1996: 288).

Campaigning in the area involved both the political parties and Scotland Forward. Labour played a key role, helping to bring Deputy Prime Minister John Prescott to Falkirk in August, accompanied by canvassing and leafleting in key local areas to mobilise support as well as a number of stalls on Saturdays before the referendum itself. Scotland Forward sought to galvanise support for Yes with a rally in Falkirk, with STUC general secretary and local figure Campbell Christie and Labour, Liberal Democrat and SNP representatives (*Falkirk Herald*, 4th September 1997: 7). The SNP ran its own campaign separately from Labour in Falkirk. Though the SNP arrived relatively late in the campaign on the ground, its efforts were organized at constituency level and, whilst it participated in a couple of public meetings, most of its time was spent door knocking to mobilise its own supporters for the referendum. Moreover, whilst both Labour and the SNP made progress in contacting voters, there was little evidence of the No campaign in the Falkirk area following the demise of the Tories at the general election.[9]

Across the River Forth in Ochil constituency (largely congruent with Clackmannanshire Council), there were two significant developments on the Yes side of the campaign. First, there was cooperation between the parties and also the involvement of the trade unions in the campaign. Scotland Forward's local campaign launched on 21st July 1997 at Alloa town hall (*Alloa Advertiser*, 25th July 1997), with the presence of Labour and trade union figures and the support of the Liberal Democrats. The SNP were present at the meeting and pledged to campaign for a Yes vote if the UK government's White Paper on devolution was positive. Shortly afterwards, Scotland Forward became active on the ground with a stall in Alloa High Street distributing leaflets, badges, balloons and pledge cards to develop support (*Alloa Advertiser*, 7th August 1997: 11). The local SNP constituency organization announced that it agreed to campaign for a Yes vote and cooperate with Scotland Forward – a move that was accompanied by the fact that local figure George Reid (SNP candidate at the 1997 general election) had joined the board of Scotland Forward. Around the same time, the local Liberal Democrat candidate Jamie Mar (the Earl of Mar and Kellie) declared support for Yes at the referendum (*Alloa Advertiser*, 28th August: 1). Mar also subsequently took part in launching cross-party campaigning with Labour MP Martin O'Neill, the SNP's George Reid and officials from trade unions Unison and the Transport and General Workers Union (*Alloa Advertiser*, 28th August 1997:12). Second, whilst cross-party efforts were symbolically important, the political parties got on with the campaigning. The SNP campaigned strongly in the Hillfoots area, where its support was strongest. Though the SNP mostly sought to mobilise its own supporters, it did notice that Labour voters were much more in favour of devolution than previously.[10] The SNP very much fought its own campaign in the 1997 referendum and its efforts were much more solid than in 1979, with more concerted door knocking and a get out the vote operation on the day. But the materials it used were centrally provided by the party rather than having any local content – at the recent general election there had been local leaflets, a local newspaper plus targeted direct mailings, but none of this was attempted at the referendum. There was no cooperation with Labour, though it was felt that the campaign did benefit from the national level of cooperation between the two parties and the positive nature of the overall campaign.[11] Whilst the Yes parties made progress – and some demonstrated a measure of common cause - Think Twice struggled. The only Conservative councillor on Clackmannanshire Council declared he would be casting this vote for a Scottish Parliament but against tax powers on referendum day, whilst the local party only managed to officially launch its Think Twice group in Alloa on 28th August (*Alloa Advertiser*, 4th September 1997: 5).

Even in areas Labour dominated historically, there was an awareness that there had to be a real campaign to deliver a Yes Yes vote at the referendum: even though the activist base had just worked through an intensive general election in the lead up to the May election. For example, pro-devolution Labour MP George Foulkes was active in the Labour campaign in his Carrick, Cumnock and Doon Valley constituency at the referendum:

> That was a very vigorous campaign, we worked really hard. We ran it effectively like a general election campaign and we got a good turnout and a good Yes vote in Carrick, Cumnock and Doon Valley. And we had meetings and leaflets and going around street meetings. Going to groups and talking to them about it. It was a very vigorous campaign (SPA/757).

Moreover, according to Foulkes and reflecting the fact that Labour was completely dominant in the constituency both in 1997 and historically:

> It was principally the Labour Party Yes Yes campaign. We did work nationally on a wider basis but in Carrick, Cumnock and Doon Valley – again in the 1997 general election my majority had gone up to 21,000 – it seems strange now but it was very Labour dominated and we had dominated every village in the constituency so it was better to run it as a Labour Party campaign effectively (SPA/757).

In some parts of Scotland, campaigning for devolution was highly problematic due to local factors – reflected in historic voting in 1979 as well as in the pattern of voting at the 1997 referendum.

For example, the sitting MP in Orkney and Shetland, Jim Wallace was both leader of the pro-devolution Liberal Democrats with a role in the national campaign and a former key member of the Scottish Constitutional Convention. However, he also had to play a role in his constituency in support of a Yes Yes vote:

> That was one of the biggest challenges because Orkney and Shetland had two of the biggest No votes in 79 and I remember in the 79 referendum watching the results coming in and Jo Grimond was being interviewed by Robin Day and the Shetland result coming in and Robin Day saying to Jo Grimond "Well there you are Mr Grimond, your constituents have said No to a Scottish Assembly just as in 1975 they said No to the European Community, two of the key policies of the Liberal Party in the last half century what do you think of that?" And Jo Grimond said "I never did think they read my election address." It was a real battle on our hands. If you look at the percentage swing from Yes to No it was a massive turnaround, which I really put an awful lot of effort into it. Things that we had got like the proportional representation system was absolutely crucial, separate seats for Orkney and Shetland was vitally important. I think there were a lot of arguments that we put forward on issues which were absolutely crucial on farming and fishing. We would have a bigger voice arguing these things in Scotland than we would have had at a Westminster level (SPA/768).

In other areas, the nature of the local campaign and its reception were mixed. Sometimes the local campaign was cross-party, in other places the parties were central. For Isobel Lindsay, in Biggar, the cross-party element was important:

> I remember we got together one of the local ministers, a local Labour councillor, Tom my husband, someone from the Lib Dems and various other people... We had quite a successful meeting down in New Lanark and we did a lot of press releases to local papers and did stalls in the local towns but it was totally different from '79 (SPA/782).

However, the different local campaigning styles of the parties were also influential in the nature of the Yes campaign delivered on the ground and which party was most involved. For Yes campaigner, Kevin Dunion, the 1997 referendum offered a challenge to party cultures in Scotland:

> I think that Labour Party activists on the ground are geared up for local elections, they have a task to do, they know what to do in terms of knocking up doors and getting the vote out for their candidate. And this is asking them to do something else. We were asking them to organise local events - I ended up speaking at church halls and school fetes. We were asking them to go out of their comfort zone. And I think the SNP and Liberals were quite used to balloon politics, they liked that kind of thing. And again I am talking from my experience, maybe it went swimmingly in other parts of Scotland. But definitely in the parts of Scotland that I went to the SNP were in the driving seat (SPA/767).

The Referendum Result and Outcome

Whilst in retrospect the local results, like the national results, were entirely predictable, it didn't seem so to Yes campaigners who remembered what had happened in 1979 all too well. Campaigners with memories had a level of positivity edged with skepticism. Certainly, there was confidence amongst some Yes campaigners about the nature of the result. At the Stirling count in the Albert Halls, local activists undertook ballot box samples but concentrated on the tax-varying powers ballot as a better measure of the likely overall result: the ballot papers for the first question on setting up a parliament were so overwhelmingly Yes, there was no point in sampling them. Whether that would be repeated across Scotland was open to question. However, Stirling had been a Conservative seat at Westminster just 4 months before the referendum so could count as a bellwether of sorts: if Think Twice were to win anywhere on referendum night it would be in places like Stirling. Referendum night was a long one but the first council to declare was Clackmannanshire Council just after midnight, which saw a Yes vote of 80 per cent for the parliament question and 68.7 per cent on the tax question on a turnout of 66.1 per cent. That result indicated that Yes supporters from Labour and the SNP had turned out, so that the various efforts at mobilizing existing Yes supporters had succeeded. Falkirk showed a similar result with a parliament Yes vote of 80 per cent and 69.2 per cent supporting tax-varying powers, on a turnout of 63.7 per cent. The Stirling result was much closer, reflecting the strength of Conservatives support in the area, with a Yes vote of 68.5 per cent for establishing a Scottish Parliament but a much lower Yes vote of and 58.9 per cent to tax-varying powers, with a turnout of 65.8 per cent.

Across Scotland, all 32 local government counting areas registered Yes votes to create a Scottish Parliament. The highest vote was in West Dunbartonshire at 84.7 per cent, followed by Glasgow, North Lanarkshire and East Ayrshire – all above 80 per cent. The lowest Yes results were in Dumfries and Galloway on 60.7 per cent and Orkney on 57.3 per cent. When it came to the tax question, Orkney voted No by 52.6 per cent to 47.4 per cent, whilst Dumfries and Galloway voted No by 51.2 per cent to 48.8 per cent. However, these were the only 2 council areas to oppose tax powers. Notably, each had shown significant movement towards devolution since 1979, as had Shetland. The highest votes in favour of tax powers came in Glasgow at 75 per cent, followed by West Dunbartonshire, North Lanarkshire and East Ayrshire. Overall, there was a clear gap in support for the parliament and tax powers in all 32 counting areas, with some of the tax vote being much more even in areas like Borders, East Renfrewshire, Perthshire and Kinross and Shetland. When all the counting areas had reported, Scotland had voted by 74.3 per cent to 25.7 per cent in support of establishing a Scottish Parliament, and by 63.5 per cent to 36.5 per cent in favour of that parliament having tax-varying powers.

Conclusion

It might be tempting to attribute the strong double Yes vote of 1997 to the more unified Yes campaign at the referendum above all else. Yes unity was one of the main aims of Scotland Forward and the parties active in the Yes campaign and their efforts were largely successful –

a unified and positive message was communicated to Labour, Liberal Democrat and SNP voters by their parties. The 1997 campaign pattern was very unlike 1979, with cooperation at the national and local levels and the parties able to do their own thing on the ground in a complementary manner. Labour on the ground was stronger and more unified in favour of the devolution proposals and the SNP was more positive and more active. The complete loss of Conservative MPs at the 1997 election removed a tier of political leadership from the party at the referendum and the election effectively demobilized the party as a serious force beyond talking to its own core supporters. Similarly, unlike in 1979, it was unprepared for the referendum and it took time for Think Twice to develop organizationally – arguably it didn't. This time around, the Conservatives were on their own in the campaign, with no significant Labour allies to oppose devolution and it was futile to try to approach Labour voters on the issue following 18 years in government.

However, more generally, public attitudes to devolution had changed in the years after 1997. Devolution was a much more solid constitutional preference amongst both elites, organisations and voters and it did not sag in opinion polls as it had in the months leading up to the 1979 referendum. Various devolution plans and schemes had been discussed after 1979, with a range of staging posts to success in 1997, such as the formation of the Campaign for a Scottish Assembly, the Claim of Right, the Scottish Constitutional Convention and the activities of a range of groups like the Calton Hill vigil, Democracy for Scotland, Common Cause and the STUC. A compromise devolution scheme was designed, but gentle campaigning and promotion of the idea of Home Rule took place regularly and did not get derailed by cross-party disputes (even though it threatened to do so at times). Finally, campaigns and campaigning aside, Scotland had changed. Home Rule had more solid voter support, Labour was more united on the issue and the Conservatives had declined. The political and economic effects of the Conservative governments from 1979-1997 had an effect on opinion. This change was not taken for granted however – hence the need for a referendum in the first place and one that was carefully managed, with two questions offered, one to neutralize the potential negativity from the income tax proposals. Mobilising the levels of support for devolution was also important –

meaning ensuring that voters actually turned up on referendum day to vote so that both the national and the local campaigns actually mattered.

Endnotes

1. Blair's own autobiography revealed a lukewarm attitude to devolution. See Tony Blair (2010), *A Journey*, London: Random House, p.251.
2. Bank of England data at http://www.bankofengland.co.uk/statistics.
3. Office of National Statistics time series data at the National Archives http://webarchive.nationalarchives.gov.uk
4. Unemployment statistics from Office of National statistics - https://www.ons.gov.uk/employmentandlabourmarket/peoplenotinwork/unemployment/timeseries/mgsx
5. Interview with local Conservative campaigner, Helen Scott, SPA/728.
6. Interview with local Conservative campaigner, John Holliday, SPA/507.
7. Interview with local SNP campaigner, Jim Thomson, SPA/747.
8. Interview with Dennis Canavan, SPA/158.
9. Interview with local SNP campaigner, David Alexander, SPA/161. Though neither Falkirk constituency was an area of strong support for the Conservatives, the party had still won around 10,000 votes across the two seats in 1997.
10. Interview with local SNP campaigner, Isobel Kindlen, SPA/171.
11. Interview with local SNP campaigner, David McCann, SPA/576.

5

The 2014 Scottish Independence Referendum

Introduction

The 2014 referendum campaign was a very different one from those that went before. Key to the 2014 referendum was the existence of devolution from 1999. It was the institution through which the referendum was pursued and implemented – through the electoral strength of the SNP at the Scottish election of 2011. Without that majority victory alongside a manifesto commitment to hold a referendum, no referendum would have occurred. However, that mandate needed to be recognized by the UK government and then negotiated through the medium of the Edinburgh Agreement in 2012 to make the referendum a reality. Both of the 1979 and 1997 referendums were instituted through legislation and rules from Westminster and, in the case of 1979, a very fraught legislative process in which the Labour Government lost control of its own policy and saw it amended by backbench opposition to include both a referendum and one that included the special 40 per cent threshold rule. The 2014 experience was completely different as the referendum was the subject of negotiation between the Scottish and UK governments to ensure it was constitutional (Scottish Government 2012), with the conclusion of an intergovernmental agreement in October 2012, followed by special arrangements to devolve the referendum issue to the Scottish Parliament. Therefore, the referendum legislation did not proceed through the House of

Commons or House of Lords, but through the Scottish Parliament. Moreover, there was two different Acts to deal with the referendum itself[1] - one to create the referendum and a second to implement a franchise extension for 16 and 17 year olds.[2] Before this, there was no framework legislation in the Scottish Parliament to guide any referendum (Electoral Commission 2014: 28). In contrast to the 1979 and 1997 experiences, the independence referendum was held under the rules and oversight of the Electoral Commission and the campaign had the novelty of pitching government against government in a UK referendum campaign for the first time. The Electoral Commission also played a role in altering the referendum question to the shortened – Should Scotland be an independent country?[3]

Why did the referendum happen? On the one hand, it was down to the SNP's unexpected electoral success in 2011, its determination to pursue the referendum and willingness to negotiate with the UK government to make it happen. On the other hand, it also required the UK government to accept the SNP's election mandate and not attempt to deny or frustrate the referendum process (which could be counter-productive) and also conduct a successful negotiation that would create a fair, legal and decisive referendum. Of course, behind this position was the political calculation that the pro-Union side would win, which would damage the SNP and derail popular support for independence: hence the determination to keep any devo max/devo reform option off of the ballot paper (Mitchell 2016: 81). Part of this view was shaped by the fact that popular support on the constitution was different at the outset of the referendum campaign. Yes began well behind at the 2014 referendum and struggled to make up ground throughout the long campaign (though it did, especially in the last month).

There were a number of other contextual factors that were significant in 2014. First, the length of the referendum campaign was staggering. The campaign effectively began with the launches of Yes Scotland in May 2012, followed quickly after by Better Together in June. However, there were a number of significant staging posts during the campaign too when voters would have been more aware of a campaign happening: like the Edinburgh Agreement, White Paper launch in November 2013 or live TV debates between Alex

Salmond and Alastair Darling in August 2014. The length of the campaign created problems for the campaigners at every level – how to sustain interest and activity for such a long period of time? For Yes, the time period was an opportunity to build and to seek opinion-reversal on the independence question (LeDuc 2002). It was also an opportunity to distance the referendum from the recession and Great Financial Crisis and also hope that some of the arguments against independence would wear out over a long campaign akin to a US Presidential election. For Better Together, the time period was difficult on the ground because it was felt its component parts could not sustain a ground campaign for very long – hence a concentration of campaigning from June 2014 onwards to September (Shaw 2014), though there was significant ground campaigning before this date. For both organisations, there was plenty of time to create their structures, raise money and design and implement their campaigns: 28 months in total. This wasn't like 1979 or 1997 though, it might not have seemed like that on the inside of the campaigns.

Second, there was variety in the campaign and the campaigning compared to 1979, 1997 and many other referendums. There was to be orthodox political campaigning (and political marketing was central to the referendum) but also more campaigning and at greater levels than usually seen in referendums or elections – with lots of new organisations and individual campaigners involved. So, campaign intensity was high (Mitchell 2016: 91) and, probably significantly higher than at general elections The social media dimension was huge – which was certainly new – but so were the types of engagement, especially by the Yes campaign: meaning there was art, music, political carnival, cartoons, poetry, etc. alongside the growing political networks and new organisations like National Collective, Radical Independence and Women for Independence. As one of National Collective's creators explained:

> National Collective provided a space for people to explore the meaning of independence outwith traditional politics, and would go on to be recognized as well as criticized, as the offhand, improvised, bohemian wing of the movement. Sometimes naïve, amateur and unpolished, it was all part of the organic quality of the Yes campaign (Barr 2016: 6).

Especially on the Yes side, there was a lot of political carnival and engagement. There was also more doorstep campaigning and community meetings too, with door and phone canvassing, lots of leafleting, debates, information evenings, etc. A host of private and public organisations advanced their own agendas in referendum debates too which Mitchell referred to as 'purposeful opportunism' (Mitchell 2016: 11), as well as sometimes providing 'advice' within their institutions. All of this fed into the unusually high level of voter registrations of 4,283,938 in total and turnout of 84.6 per cent (Electoral Commission 2014: 59). There were also mini-campaigns by prominent political figures – like Jim Murphy's 100 town tour of Scotland (see Geoghegan 2015: 143-8), Gordon Brown's book (Brown 2014), public speaking tour and newspaper articles late in the campaign, Tommy Sheridan's *Hope Over Fear* public meeting tour, George Galloway's *Just Say Naw* events or Jim Sillars' use of the Margo Mobile to visit Scotland's working class communities (as discussed in chapter 2.

Third, the scope of issues was large and potentially endless. What this meant is that every issue was discussable at the independence referendum including - perhaps especially - the unknowable future. So, the economy, currency, pensions, identity, the constitution, devolution reform, environment, fairness, democracy, defence and international affairs, the EU, agriculture and fishing, the BBC, the lottery, tax and spending, immigration, culture, etc., were all featured in the campaign along with many other issues as the independence issue threw so many basic questions and issues up into the air. Campaign groups tried to generate broad themes to deal with this or to link certain issues into their campaign, but for campaigners on the ground the variety was challenging: especially for Yes campaigners who were the ones proposing change and had to field questions on every topic under the sun. Nonetheless, the length and intensity of the campaign and the multiple issues at stake brought a lot of ordinary people to engage with the issues through the media and discussion with families and friends.

Fourth, though the ballot paper asked a binary question, behind No was the prospect of further devolution.[4] This factor was an echo of 1979, when the Conservatives offered the hope of an improved devolution scheme in Alec Douglas-Home's TV interview. Before the

2014 referendum, the Conservatives, Labour and Liberal Democrats had published alternative plans for Scottish devolution (Scottish Conservative Party 2014; Scottish Labour Devolution Commission 2014: Scottish Liberal Democrats 2012, 2014) and these featured prominently in the campaign – indicating how Scotland could get the best of both worlds through economic security in the UK and a strong devolved parliament. It was these proposals that formed the basis of the Vow, printed on the front page of the *Daily Record* on 16th September 2014 when all three UK party leaders came to Scotland to galvanise the No vote – intended to link No and more devolution more markedly (Liñera, Henderson and Delaney 2017: 169). However, whilst the Vow was a late moment of drama – aimed largely at Labour voters [5]– the fact that No did not mean 'no change' for Scotland had been trailed for some considerable time. Because of this, the binary choice was not really a binary choice at all. The issue of a third option on the ballot paper – that of devolution reform – had been discussed in 2007 and again in 2012 but nothing concrete emerged. The UK government and pro-Union parties ruled out having a devolution reform alternative on the ballot paper against independence, allowing Yes to claim that it meant they weren't serious about more devolution and a strong option like devo-max.[6] However this position did not survive 2014 as the Better Together parties sought to reframe No as a reform option in advance of the referendum itself to broaden the appeal of a No vote to independence. The fact that the three parties produced different sets of proposals – and in Labour's case, one that lacked coherence on taxation – was seen to be less important than the fact that they all promised more devolution: a core message of the Better Together campaign and its claim that Scotland had the best of both worlds.

Economic and Political Context

The political environment of the independence referendum was a very mixed one for both sides in the campaign with contrasting shaping factors. On the one hand, there was a majority SNP government in Edinburgh, able to implement its plans for an independence referendum, use the government machinery to support its independence prospectus and try to shape political events to help its case. On the other hand, the larger UK government was in the same position to use its machinery against independence and in support of the Union, as well as generate sympathetic statements from international politicians. It was comprised of a coalition of the Conservatives and Liberal Democrats and often much more capable of making the political weather than the Scottish Government. It published 16 different Scotland Analysis papers during the referendum, which set out the UK's position on the issues and drove significant media coverage for the pro-Union side. The parliaments also offered contrasting fortunes for the campaigns, with the Better Together parties able to utilize the committees of the House of Commons and Lords to promote their case, with Yes having supportive committee inquiries by the Scottish Parliament (Adamson and Lynch 2014: 53-4).

The political party dimension of the referendum campaign was also important though. The fact that it was a Conservative-led coalition, with the Prime Minister, Chancellor of the Exchequer etc., implementing spending cuts certainly helped the Yes campaign. The dynamic of anti-Conservative Scotland versus a Conservative-led UK government was politically useful, as was Labour's diminished position in Scottish and UK politics: something which was much more obvious after the referendum, at least up until the party's partial recovery at the general election in June 2017. In party terms, Yes was supported by one major party – the SNP – as well as two minor parties, the Scottish Green Party and Scottish Socialist Party. Better Together was supported by the Conservatives, Labour and Liberal Democrats, who were notionally able to mobilise more voters, activists, finance and media support for their cause in Scotland as well as across the UK.

Opinion poll support for the political parties in Scotland provided a very mixed picture throughout the referendum campaign. Part of the reason for this was the continuation of differential voting at Scottish and UK elections. This practice showed that the SNP was strong at Holyrood elections but weak at Westminster elections, whilst Labour arguably was the complete reverse (not every opinion poll showed this pattern though). This reality produced conflicting pictures during the referendum campaign – of a strong and dominant SNP in Scottish Parliament opinion polling, alongside a strong and dominant Labour Party in Westminster opinion polling, with electoral politics seemingly dominated by these two parties. For example, Labour led in Westminster opinion polls for most of the referendum campaign period, though was behind the SNP except for a few months in the late summer/early autumn of 2011 and then in April-June 2014. In referendum month itself, Labour was polling between 39 per cent and 43 per cent, with the SNP fluctuating between 22 per cent and 35 per cent.[7]

Opinion polls for Scottish elections showed a more SNP-dominant picture 2011-2014. The party won 45.4 per cent on the constituency vote at the 2011 election and 44 per cent on the regional list vote. Its opinion poll rating on the constituency vote was remarkably consistent during the referendum period. It moved from 42 per cent in May 2011 up to 49 per cent in August and was frequently above 40 per cent during the referendum campaign. Support dipped below that level in May and September 2013, in June 2014 (where it polled 35 per cent and 46 per cent in the same month) and then levels of 39 per cent, 36 per cent and 37 per cent in August 2014, some of its lowest polling during the campaign. In September 2014, opinion poll support for the SNP moved up to 39 per cent and 40 per cent just before the referendum: before support spiraled even higher after the referendum loss.[8] Support for Labour at Holyrood over the period began on highs of 41 per cent in February and March 2011 but actual support declined to 31.7 per cent of the constituency vote and 26.3 per cent of the regional list vote at the May 2011 Scottish election. After the election, the party tended to poll above 30 per cent but seldom overtook the SNP. It did so in September 2013 when it polled 39 per cent to the SNP's 31 per cent and then again in January 2013 with 38 per cent. Labour managed to lead the SNP again in August 2014 with 37 per cent to 36 per cent.[9] However, come referendum month, Labour was second to the SNP in Holyrood polling preferences.

Opinion poll support for Scottish independence was generally low during the referendum campaign – at least compared to support for the No option. It was the No campaign that held consistent and compelling opinion poll leads for most of the referendum and at times, it looked like it would achieve a crushing victory. The 2011 Scottish Election Survey provided two different measures of constitutional support. It asked a five-option question on constitutional preferences, which found 26 per cent support for independence (in or out of the EU), 63 per cent support for devolution (with or without tax powers) and 12 per cent favouring no parliament at all (Carman, Johns and Mitchell 2014: 99). A three option question between independence, more devolution powers and the status quo found 24 per cent support for independence, 38 per cent for more powers and 38 per cent for the existing devolution settlement (Carman, Johns and Mitchell 2014: 99). In short, Yes came from a very low starting point in 2011. For a time, opinion polling used both Yes/No options on independence as well as more complex polling questions that encompassed devolution reform options. However, most polls showed gaps in support that gave No healthy leads over Yes and Yes only occasional leads. So, that side of the campaign faced an uphill struggle throughout the referendum – the fact it ended the campaign with higher support than at the beginning was significant though.

Just as at other referendums, government and politics went on around the independence referendum – with every decision and event assessed for its relevance for the referendum. There were two sets of elections between the 2011 Scottish election trigger and the 18th September 2014 – with the local elections of May 2012 and the European election of June 2014. Both Labour and the SNP polled well as the local elections, with the SNP ahead on first preferences with 32.33 per cent and Labour in second place on 31.39 per cent, with both parties increasing their councillor numbers. Significantly though, Labour held off the SNP in Glasgow to retain control. The period also saw three by-elections for the Scottish Parliament – the SNP comfortably held Aberdeen Donside in June 2013 but lost Dunfermline to Labour in October 2013 and saw Labour comfortably retain Cowdenbeath in January 2014. The latter two contests were significant as they took place in areas of Labour-SNP contestation at the electoral level but also, at the referendum level between Yes and Better Together: though neither contests could be seen as surrogates for the referendum.[10] At the European Parliament election, the SNP retained its first place with 29 percent of the vote and 2 MEPs, with Labour in second place with 25.9 per cent of the vote and 2 MEPs.

The remaining two positions were divided between the Conservatives on 17.2 per cent and UKIP on 10.5 per cent. The Greens missed out despite a decent performance of 8.1 per cent, just ahead of the Liberal Democrats on 7.1 per cent.

The economic environment around the independence referendum was shaped by the Great Financial Crisis that began in 2008 with the collapse of Lehman Brothers in the USA. The crisis had both specific and all-encompassing effects on the referendum environment. EU member states like Greece, Ireland, Portugal and Cyprus required financial bailouts, whilst Spain required a special financial mechanism from the EU. The crisis effected UK banking significantly, with major bailouts of Scottish banks such as Bank of Scotland (HBOS) and the Royal Bank of Scotland. In time, this led to bank restructuring and redundancies in Scotland. Banking bailouts were one of the reasons for the increased level of government borrowing during these years, with a general strain on public finances with UK Government austerity policies. In a country with an internationalized economy and a considerable financial sector, the GFC and its various components was a highly negative shaping factor for the independence campaign and also a considerable campaign gift to Better Together, which would frame some of its campaign around security, uncertainty and the pooling of risk and reward within existing UK structures plus Scottish economic weakness (see Lecca, MacGregor and Swales 2017; Swan and Petersohn 2017). Some of this was effective because of the negative economic environment and appealed to risk-averse voters in particular (though not enough to prevent support for Yes increasing) (Liñeira, Henderson and Delaney 2017). Yes struggled to de-risk the economics of independence though sought to frame its economic arguments positively, whilst Better Together could focus on economic risk based on recent examples that had been prominent and sometimes ongoing in the media since 2007 – and examples that struck right into the Scottish employment market and business community.

The economic crisis also produced record low interest rates at 0.5 per cent from 5th March 2009 onwards, throughout the referendum campaign and beyond. This was one indication of the emergency measures adopted by the Bank of England and the UK Government to deal with the crisis – essentially to make borrowing cheaper and easier and give mortgage holders more money in their pockets to spend to boost economic activity (and hope to stave off house repossessions). UK unemployment rose during the early years of the GFC before declining in 2014. For example, UK unemployment stood at 5.2 per cent in January-March 2008 rising to 7.9 per cent from May to July 2009 and then upwards to 8.4 per cent from October to December 2011 before falling to 6 per cent August-October 2014.[11] In Scotland, unemployment was 6.9 per cent in 2009, rising to 8.2 per cent in 2011, then 7.7 per cent in 2013 and 6.2 per cent in 2014.[12] Finally, inflation became an economic problem for consumers as it rose from 3.4 per cent in March 2009 to 5.2 per cent in September 2010, before falling beneath 2 per cent in January 2014 and down to 1.2 per cent by September 2014.[13]

The National Campaign

The 2014 independence referendum took place under the aegis of the Electoral Commission – established by the Political Parties, Elections and Referendums Act of 2000. The organization provided a framework of rules and regulations for 2014 as well as designating lead campaigners and providing official status to a host of campaign groups (many groups were required to register officially and produce spending returns). Not surprisingly, Yes Scotland and Better Together were designated as the official lead campaign organisations and this involved setting out agreed spending limits and rules about their activities. A key point about spending regulation was that it applied to the official regulated period of 30th May 2014 to 18th September 2014: spending before then did not count. So, the official figures cited here are for the last few months of the campaign, even though organisations spent considerable sums on the referendum before this date. In addition, the regulations applied to specific things like campaign materials, advertising, market research, campaign broadcasts, rallies and press conferences - not to staff costs, volunteers, food and accommodation whilst campaigning (Electoral Commission 2015: 10). The Electoral Commission regulations meant that the two main campaign groups were limited to spending £1.5 million each in the official campaign period. Better Together spent £1,422,602, whilst Yes Scotland spent £1,420,800, whilst amongst the parties, the SNP spent £1,298,567, Labour spent £732,482, the Conservatives spent £356,191, the Liberal Democrats spent £187,585 and the Greens spent £13,734 (Electoral Commission 2015: 12). Other Yes and No groups also spent considerable sums – for example for Yes, Business for Scotland spent £143,027, National Collective spent £54,849 and Women for Independence spent £24,605, whilst for No, the No Borders organization spent £147,510, the Orange Lodge spent £47,072 and the GMB spent £43,385 (Electoral Commission 2015: 48-9). When it came to donations - which are also regulated by the Electoral Commission – the No campaign was much more effectively financed compared to Yes. Donations to the various No campaign bodies totaled £4,327,677, compared to £2,990,868 for Yes (Electoral Commission 2015: 16). The pattern of donations to the No side indicated that a large number of small donors had supported the campaign, with a third of donations coming from the small donors, compared to only 8 per cent for Yes (Electoral commission 2015: 20). Yes was rather reliant on the big donations that came from the Euromillions winners, the Weirs, as well as from the SNP (though there were a lot of localized crowdfunding efforts too). There were a total of 42 registered groups in 2014, 21 for Yes and 21 for No.[14]

To some extent, both Better Together and Yes Scotland faced quite similar challenges during the referendum as they created extensive political marketing campaigns. Each had to create offices and hire staff, raise money and design their campaigns but also deal with party conflict within their coalitions. Some of the problems they faced were a result of friendly fire and their supporters telling them what to do – the amount of time Better Together staff spent dealing with disputes between and within their political parties could fill a book (there were shades of the 1979 and 1997 devolution referendum campaigns here). Each campaign had to manage media relations, governments, parties, a range of different economic and social interests as well listen to a host of participants and observers telling them they were doing campaigning wrong. Each conducted research on voter attitudes to constitutional change and also, to some extent, designed their campaigns to attract middle voters on the issue – meaning the soft Yes and No voters and the undecided (see Liñera, Henderson and Delaney 2017): all parts of the campaign focused on these as well as signing up supporters and campaigners (through Nationbuilder, the Yes Declaration, paid reply leaflets, public meetings, stalls, etc.).[15] For Better Together, the most significant element of their campaign – and its tone and messaging – was directed at the undecideds (Shorthouse 2015) and fending off Yes Scotland's efforts in converting soft No voters to independence. Each side used celebrities as well as ordinary people (or campaigners appearing as ordinary people) to carry their messages for them. In the case of Yes, this often involved people telling of their journey to Yes. The point about both celebrities and ordinary people was to attempt to reach voters without the involvement of politicians and parties, each of which was seen to be untrusted to some extent. Instead, the campaigns looked to use people and issues that were 'relatable'. Yes Scotland's campaign as a whole was built upon the idea of conversations and conversions through family, friends and the work place not through big events like the TV debates or the launch of the Scottish Government's White Paper in November 2013 (though ironically, the big event approach was as prominent as the grassroots conversations at times).

Before looking at the two campaign groups and their local activities, it's worth remembering that perfect campaigns only exist on paper. Every campaign faces obstacles in terms of resources, changing circumstances, events, miscalculations and mistakes, the activities of opponents, etc. So, whilst we can point to some of the things Better Together and Yes Scotland did wrong – and focus on the things that went wrong – lots of things actually went right too. So, in amongst the party in-fighting within and between the Better Together parties, the campaign organization produced a winning campaign to shore up a lot of the existing No vote as well as ensuring a lot of undecided voters opted for the Union. Yes Scotland faced all sorts of financial and staffing problems and real pressure on its capacity as a central organization but it actually succeeded in its strategy of creating a huge grassroots campaign and increasing support for independence from a comparatively low base before the campaign began.

Yes Scotland

Yes Scotland was formed and launched in May 2012. Initially, it was staffed by a small team in Edinburgh before transferring to a larger permanent office in Glasgow's Hope Street which opened on 19th November 2012. Its Chief Executive Blair Jenkins was one of the few permanent staff members from foundation to the referendum, but had no campaign or election-fighting experience. Many of the staff who joined Yes Scotland as directors or deputy directors early in the organisation's life were gone by the time of the referendum – all five senior directors had left the organisation by early 2014, as had some of the deputy directors. These changes were indicative of a lack of funding for the organization, a lack of direction at times and a lot of internal conflict and dissatisfaction. Staff turnover also cost money and damaged morale – and it did not create confidence amongst the grassroots Yes community either. From beginning to end, Yes Scotland was weak when it came to the electoral side of campaigning, with a poorly organized office and no clear campaign plan in place (if they had one, they didn't share it internally or with campaigners). It continually struggled to raise money and lacked a proper fundraising strategy. The organisation had a £496,525 deficit at the end of the campaign and it required two SNP bailouts to save it - £275,000 in September 2014 and £550,000 in November 2014.[16] In spite of these difficulties, the grassroots Yes campaign did develop. As Yes Scotland staff member Stephen Noon pointed out in 2014:

> Right from the launch of Yes Scotland, almost two years ago, we knew our best chance of winning the referendum was to create the biggest grassroots movement in Scotland's history.........The core concept behind our social campaign is the idea of 'conversion through conversation', with our enthusiastic and informed volunteers and supporters becoming the primary advocates and ambassadors for a Yes. Each one holding a series of conversations with people in their social networks, breaking the issues around independence into manageable, bite sized chunks and then nudging people up the support scale from unconvinced or undecided to a clear Yes (Noon 2014).

What Yes Scotland sought to do – via traditional media, social media, advertising, messaging and grassroots activity – was pursue a three-step campaign on the issue of democracy, fairness and a wealthy Scotland, to move voters from awareness of the referendum, to consider the issues around independence versus the Union and then to make a decision in favour of independence. The idea was to move voters up the 1-10 scale of support for independence, through getting them to consider the reasons for independence, the costs of Union, the gains to come from a Yes vote and the consequences of a No vote. Doing this through a grassroots campaign was intended to help Yes to compete with the fact the media would be hostile to independence and allow Better Together an inbuilt advantage. The campaign contained a lot of optimistic messages, soft nationalism and nationbuilding, all intended to make voters open to thinking about independence and effectively normalizing independence as a constitutional option in Scotland for the first time. How did Yes attempt to achieve this? Partly through social media messages and infographics (see Bremner 2015), partly through the establishment of a large number of sectoral groups for Yes who could speak to different and distinct audiences (farmers, youth, Poles, fishing). Some of the messaging was issue-based, some ideological – so there were messages directed at Green voters, Labour voters, liberals, etc., and anti-Conservative messages too. The Labour electorate was one of particular contestation by Yes, aided by a Labour for Independence[17] group though one that was too small and lacked senior figures from the party. Yes tended to be reliant on older Labour voices and formerly prominent Labour figures rather than current figures – despite the regular speculation about former First Minister Henry McLeish coming out for Yes (he didn't). On the ground, it had something like 173 local groups by the end of 2012 (Torrance 2013: 259) and around 300 by the time the referendum was held.

The organizational weakness of Yes Scotland contrasted with the ambitions in some of its early planning. The Yes strategic business plan – *Winning Independence* – was leaked to the media after the referendum. It had the goal of raising £24 million, 65 per cent support for Yes and five pro-Yes newspapers by the time of the referendum,[18] the creation of an independent economic think tank that supported independence, the training of 500 media influencers, plus local Yes offices and shops all over Scotland (local groups actually created these independently of the central organisation). There was talk of Yes Scotland being decentralised into 6 regions, with full-time local organizers and a 150 staff but none of this transpired. Instead, Yes struggled to raise funds and resource the grassroots campaign that developed beneath it, often in an autonomous way (local groups had no choice but to self-organise). Simple things like working on postal voting, electoral registration and the GOTV on the day were low priorities at Yes Scotland, partly due to lack of staff, funds and understanding, but also due to the weakness of the Yesmo database purchased for the campaign. It did function in a limited way but wasn't a sophisticated campaign device linking to demographics and voter conversion, leaving Yes with poor data from patchy canvassing and limited awareness of the electorate and of key voting groups (McAlpine 2016: 69-79; Dommett and Black 2016). Adoption of the Nationbuilder programme was intended to supplement electoral activity by making it easier to sign up volunteers, complete and process Yes declarations and promote campaign activities for volunteers, but it was also a problematic programme to operate.[19] One of the few post-referendum analyses of Yes Scotland by Common Weal founder Robin McAlpine identified a host of problems with Yes - with its strategy, management and goal of seeking to win a referendum during the campaign. For McAlpine, the Yes Scotland advisory board was weak – it actually needed an experienced management board – and it had weak voter targeting and a limited understanding of the electorate and poor canvassing planning and implementation (McAlpine 2016: 65-72). Grassroots electoral work was largely left to the local groups and lack of resourcing of the Communities section of Yes Scotland didn't help them function effectively.

Of course, Yes Scotland was only one part of the Yes campaign. The SNP's role was significant – it had extensive electoral and campaign experience – and its staff and resources assisted the campaign throughout. The party's strategy of positive campaigning - adopted at the 2007 Scottish election onwards – was also highly influential in the tone and content of Yes Scotland messaging throughout, with confidence-building and nation-building messages ('What would you say to living in one the world's wealthiest countries?' and 'Scotland helped invent the modern world. Surely we can prosper in it'). Regular contact between the party, Yes Scotland and Scottish Government special advisors helped coordinate campaign and media activities throughout. In addition, the SNP had local organization, money, grassroots campaigners and a strong centre – which saw the gaps in Yes Scotland's activities plugged by the SNP such as the Yes newspapers that appeared in the campaign. The SNP assisted with the electoral database and used its own membership to distribute campaign materials and coordinate activities. The Greens centrally and locally were active – though often in relatively small numbers – but launched their own Green Yes campaign and ran a strong social media campaign in the last months of the referendum. The SSP meantime were more active in the Radical Independence Campaign, which ran a range of activities across Scotland along with groups like Women for Independence, National Collective, Business for Scotland, Christians for Independence, etc. In any case, all the Yes parties had to spend time trying to convert their own supporters to vote for independence in 2014, whilst also relying on supporters of other parties to vote Yes to win the referendum - so simple party cues were insufficient (Mitchell 2016: 84).

Better Together

Better Together was launched on 25th June 2012 through a cross-party event at Edinburgh's Napier University. It was led by former Labour Chancellor of the Exchequer Alastair Darling - an Edinburgh MP - and directed by Labour campaigner Blair McDougall. Key figures from across the three pro-Union parties had agreed to establish the organization in April and it began as a private company with only a couple of staff in a rented office in Glasgow. Its name, messaging and framing of the referendum debate was intended to produce a positive campaign frame – based upon devolution, identity, history and ideas like mutual strength and support through pooling and sharing of resources, linked to the economy, security and public services.[20] It wasn't all negative campaigning by any means, despite the *Project Fear* label and topics employed. Compared to Yes Scotland, Better Together had more success in establishing a permanent central organisation and raising sufficient finance for the campaign

– though it might not have seemed like that at the time according to two post-mortems by journalists (Cochrane 2015, Pike 2015). At times it struggled to raise funds – even when paying fundraisers – yet its core research and messaging work was key to the campaign. Quite often, its main problems were created by partisan conflict amongst its component parts and briefings to the press – though political damage from referring to itself as 'Project Fear' was entirely self-inflicted. Better Together staff were permanently engaged in managing parties, governments, local groups etc., and trying to convince this wide array of people that its campaign design was going to prove effective despite skepticism from the professional politicians (newspapers regularly covered these types of stories). Getting the parties to work together - despite their differences - was one of its challenges, both centrally and on the ground and to prevent party divisions from damaging the campaign: real echoes of Scotland Forward in the 1996-7 period but hugely magnified by the pressure of the campaign, the issue at stake and the destructive potential of a 24 news media and social media.

Voter research was a key part of Better Together activity during the referendum. It devoted a huge amount of money and time to researching the electorate on what was a relatively new issue and its research continued up to the referendum to monitor changes in attitude and support. It spent around £800,000 on opinion polling with Populus polling company, with polls throughout the long campaign (Pike 2015: 18). One thing Populus did was to help Better Together's focus on the middle voters, those who were soft or undecided.[21] Extensive Populus surveying divided the Scottish electorate into 6 categories – mature status quo and hard-pressed Unionists (37 per cent who were most committed to the UK), the Blue collar Bravehearts and Scottish exceptionalists (29 per cent who were pro-independence) and the undecided/uncommitted groups the comfortable pragmatists and the uncommitted security seekers (34 per cent of the electorate) (Pike 2015: 18). As mentioned above, it was these middle groups that Better Together sought to focus on (Shorthouse 2015), something which caused some difficulties with the pro-Union parties. Populus focus groups were regularly convened – on reactions to the Governor of the Bank of England's visit to meet Alex Salmond on 29th January 2014, (Pike 2015: 53), on themes around risk and uncertainty and on the types of language to be used to most effect during the campaign (Pike 2015: 57-8) as both sides in the constitutional debate contested concepts like fairness, sovereignty, etc. (Adamson and Lynch 2014). Part of what Better Together sought to do was to sketch out its own campaign using the Populus data but also, to sketch out how Yes Scotland would present its campaign and messages at the referendum (Pike 2015: 59).

What Better Together did with its data pile was significant – it shaped its messages and positions on a range of themes for the duration of the campaign. It found its way into thousands of direct mail letters sent to voters as part of a campaign to contact voters like pensioners and families directly. It also went into emails harvested from voter contacts gained directly or from people who visited its website (by planting cookies on their machines – this was before EU regulations required a legal statement on data sharing on web pages) and through organisational efforts by Blue State Digital to create networks of activists and supporters. The research-based messaging was also found in its Facebook posts and tweets, in leaflets, its website, posters, youtube films, adverts and training packs: even to its controversial referendum broadcast 'The Woman who made up her mind' which was widely spoofed by Yessers but originated in a focus group conversation (Pike 2015: 111). Even when it moved from Better Together to 'No Thanks' as its main slogan, the change was focus group tested and found to be positive (Pike 2015: 74). In the latter stage of the campaign, its messaging became 'Love Scotland, Vote No" and then 'Vote No for Faster, Better, Safer Change.'

Better Together also had the benefit of existing voter data collected over the years by the political parties plus the new voter data it was collecting directly through doorstep and telephone canvassing.[22] This allowed either the parties themselves or Better Together to contact voters and link to them through party loyalties and for the parties to have voters to target on their own. Better Together canvassing asked for voters to volunteer their normal party preference at elections - unlike Yes Scotland - and this allowed the campaign to shape its messaging and provide the parties with more data to target their efforts. In essence, this meant there were two types of campaigning on the ground – that by Better Together through its own organized events and activities but also those by the three political parties. Some of the ground campaigning at the referendum was shared between the parties and folded into normal party campaigning. So, the three political parties bolted on the BT message to their leaflets, campaign materials and communications during the long campaign, including at the European election. Local parties that were active in canvassing and leafleting generally or in target seats for the 2015 UK general election included BT material and publicity in their activities too to provide an overlapping, party-specific message for No.

The Local Campaign

The level and intensity of local campaigning at the referendum was striking though difficult to quantify overall. For Better Together, local activism helped with maintaining their majority support in opinion polls and ensuring it turned out to vote. For Yes, there were rather different challenges – in terms of ensuring its supporters were registered to vote in the first place (see Sullivan 2014) and turned out to vote on the day but also, because it lagged in the polls, its task was one of conversion on the doorsteps and in homes to try to move voters towards independence.

The local political landscape for the independence referendum was quite different to 1979 and 1997 and reflected the reality of a much stronger SNP presence in central Scotland. The SNP's success at the 2011 Scottish election saw the party win all of the Holyrood constituency seats in the area, with increased support compared to 2007. The SNP held Falkirk West but increased its vote to 55.3 per cent. It also retained Stirling and saw its vote rise to 48.9 per cent. In Clackmannanshire and Dunblane, it retained the seat and its vote rose to 48.3 per cent. Finally, the SNP gained Falkirk East from Labour with 50.8 per cent. Whilst the Holyrood picture for the SNP was extremely rosy – and contributed to its independence referendum majority – its Westminster performance in 2010 had been limited. Labour comfortably held the Stirling seat in 2010 with 41.8 per cent, with the SNP languishing in third place on 17.3 per cent and the Greens on 1.6 per cent. In Ochil and South Perthshire (which included Clackmannanshire), Labour retained the seat in 2010 with 37.9 per cent to the SNP's second place

27.6 per cent: Labour's vote increased here, whilst that of the SNP fell. Finally, in Falkirk, Labour won in 2010 with 45.7 per cent to the SNP's 30.3 per cent (which was actually an increase from 2005). The local picture was one of a Labour-SNP duopoly, though in the context of a cross-party referendum, this was misleading as there were significant groups of votes for the other main parties too. And, in the case of the Conservatives, local parties were reactivated by the referendum experience as the contest gave the local members a clear and unequivocal focus for campaigning that would help galvanise their supporters as the period of 'banal activism' came to an end (Smith 2011). Significantly, this referendum saw a huge amount of local campaigning and activist mobilisation by both sides. It not only involved the parties but also brought in new activists with their own organisations and initiatives, some of them highly individualized, some as part of broader initiatives.

Yes Scotland on the Ground

The early formation of Yes Scotland on 25th May 2012 helped to generate local campaigning. Nascent local groups began to form around council areas and parliamentary constituencies with the aim of participating in a national campaign day on 23rd June. Significantly, some of these groups continued to develop and were already operational by the time Yes Scotland announced in July that it would undertake a tour of all 32 local council areas to help establish local campaign groups. This tour began on 28th September in Stornoway and wound its way through all other council areas to finish in Airdrie on 10th December. The presentations by Yes Scotland at these events were relatively broad – the aim was group formation, networking and a boost to local activism. There wasn't a campaign plan in place or any great direction about what to do, so local groups were largely left to their own devices. One focus from the launch of Yes Scotland had been the collection of signatures for the Yes declaration and this was one activity local groups undertook as well as providing (limited) information on independence and discussing the issue with the public through street stalls. Yes wanted to identify lead volunteers in each area and to have volunteers undertake ambassador training, though it's difficult to say whether this latter activity was particularly successful. One feature of the grassroots effort was the informal nature of local Yes groups – which was encouraged. The intention was not to have local groups governed by constitutions and local committees, as formality was felt to hinder local activity and end up with the groups lost in bureaucracy and committee meetings. But informality also hindered fundraising, rental of offices, etc., so wasn't always an advantage.

Yes Stirling was one of the earliest active local Yes groups. It sought to use events and stalls to generate interest. Yes Stirling began with informal meetings between a small group of local political activists and a presentation about the possible campaign to Stirling's SNP constituency association meeting in June 2012. The presentation sought to map out the different campaign periods available to the Yes side if the referendum was to be held late in 2014 (which was an educated guess), how a Yes community could be created locally with Yes groups for the different communities in Stirling Council area and also what lessons could be learned from the two previous constitutional referendums held in Scotland. The small group met on a number of occasions in 2012 and 2013 to steer the local organization before it became more formal and took on a life of its own. It outlined a hyper-local campaign plan that sought local Yes groups within the various towns and communities across the large Stirling Council area – which eventually meant groups such as Yes Dunblane, Yes Bridge of Allan, Yes Drymen, Yes Doune and Deanston and Yes Kippen. The intention was that local volunteers would then run the campaign in their area, with canvassing and leafleting on the ground, rather than try to run the campaign centrally from Stirling city. The group's first public activities were to host a Yes Scotland stall in Stirling town centre on 23rd June 2012: the first of many local stalls and activities, sometimes alternating between Stirling and Bridge of Allan and linking with the local group in Dunblane. The stalls were used for signature collection for the Yes Declaration, distributing Yes campaign material and handing out the local newsletter to help create a network of activists and supporters from the ground up. The local organization was already functioning before Yes Scotland's national tour to create local groups landed in Stirling on 4th October. It had begun to create a local email network of supporters, followed by a local e-newsletter from April 2013 onwards to grow support and coordinate campaigning (Yes Stirling 2013), and held a series of talks at the Burgh café in Stirling in January to April 2013 to gently gather support – with talks by Dennis Canavan, John Swinney, Tasmina Ahmed-Sheikh and Louise Bachelor of the Greens. It began leafleting and canvassing early compared to other groups, with the first canvass session in Doune on 15th May 2013. Yes Stirling was active on the doorsteps before the Yes Scotland database was operational and over the space of the next 18 months, it collected data on over 20,000 voters across the Stirling area: visiting and revisiting communities to find voters in key areas and ensure they were registered to vote. Yes Stirling also organised a Get out the Vote operation for referendum day itself, with local areas allocated to key campaigners to manage. The existence of a large pro-Yes student body at Stirling University was also helpful – with the student Yes group being highly active on campus amongst the student population but also providing a range of activists for wider campaign activities in Stirling as well. The students organized at fresher's weeks and held stalls on campus during the semester too, asking students to sign their own large version of the Yes Declaration (which is now in the Scottish Political Archive). The local Yes group created a Stirling Yes shop and a campaign hub via local online crowdfunders.[23] It hosted a series of meeting to publicise its cause and generate support – with Stirling as the focus for a variety of Yes activities from National Collective's local group and the Yestival tour, public meetings with Blair Jenkins and Dennis Canavan, Radical Independence meetings at the Smith Art gallery and Museum, visits from the Spirit of Independence fire engine and various other national events.

Yes Falkirk developed following the example of events by nascent Yes groups in surrounding areas. Yes Falkirk's lead volunteer had attended the Yes launch in Edinburgh in 2012 and was keen to develop a cross-party and non-party approach to the campaign locally. Initially, this meant attending early events in Stirling and Bathgate before forming Yes Falkirk and creating a variety of local Yes groups for the various communities around Falkirk.[24] The lead volunteer had a knack for social media and organization and had the benefit of not being one of the sitting SNP MSPs or councillors – and the local SNP stood back from the campaign early on. Contact was made with the Yes Scotland communities group and this led to the creation of Yes Falkirk and to the formation of a range of Yes groups in the Falkirk area bit by bit, with regular stalls and campaigning as the grass roots campaign developed. Like Stirling, Yes Falkirk was up and running before the Yes Scotland autumn tour to create local groups which arrived in Falkirk on 22nd October 2012. In time there was Yes Braes, Yes Falkirk, Yes Grangemouth, Yes Bo'ness (which crowdfunded a Yes shop),[25] Yes Stenhousemuir and Larbert (which had the Forward Stenhousemuir community hub) and Yes Bonnybridge. Structurally, the Yes groups tended to follow the ward pattern of the local government electoral districts in an electorally competitive area between Labour and the SNP, with some strong long-term SNP organisation in the area. Regular street stalls were held in Falkirk and Grangemouth, with the Falkirk stall often operational all day on Saturdays, by the steeple in the centre of the town. The stall handed out information, collected signatures for the Yes declaration and undertook some voter registration work. Yes Falkirk had their own magazine - Scotland 2014 - which was distributed from the stall in October 2013, with articles from prominent campaigners plus key facts about independence (Yes Falkirk 2013). The group bought its own merchandise – thousands of Yes wrist bands – and sold them to raise funds for the campaign. A number of the street stalls had collecting tins and constant donations helped to provide the money to buy campaign materials. The campaigns across Falkirk were run from peoples' homes and garages. As the various groups undertook voter identification work, they ended up with a team of 12-15 data processors and large local teams of regular canvassers across the 9 council wards, which canvassed approximately 3,000-4,000 voters per ward. Canvassing occurred from Mondays to Thursdays most weeks, with regular canvassing in most areas plus occasional mass canvasses to have more local impact (in Camelon and Denny for example). The mass canvasses were particularly effective in generating new campaigners, with high numbers of participants and helped to train campaigners in canvassing techniques. Whilst this level of engagement was high, with a core group of canvassers who would do 3 sessions a week, there was definitely a post-referendum feeling that more doorstep work would have helped.

Yes groups organised a range of public events across the wider council area, featuring Dennis Canavan, Blair Jenkins, Rosie Kane, Robin McAlpine, Allan Grogan, Carolyn Leckie, Jim Sillars, Colin Fox, Sandra Webster and Alan Bissett amongst others. The presence of Canavan – an extremely popular former Labour MP and Independent MSP – was particularly helpful, as it provided an entry point into the Labour electorate. There were meetings in Denny, Falkirk, Grangemouth, Tamfourhill, Hallglen, plus involvement in the debates at the Central Scotland Sensory Centre in Camelon and the *Falkirk Herald* referendum debate in the Trinity Church in the centre of Falkirk (*Falkirk Herald*, 29th May 2014). However, genuine debates to speak with undecideds were rare, meaning that Yes campaigners often found they were talking to existing supporters at meetings. Other groups were also involved in the local campaign with an active Women for Independence group plus the Radical Independence Campaign involved in canvassing Camelon and Grangemouth in June 2014. Yes Falkirk were active at Forth Valley College fresher's week in September 2013, with Generation Yes taking over this function on 4th September 2014. There was some Green involvement in the local campaign, with a number of Green Yes leaflets delivered, but neither the Greens nor Labour for Independence were particularly active in the area. Finally, on referendum day itself, there was a Get out the Vote operation localized by ward, with coordinated transport arrangements and door knocking. There was a huge turnout of volunteers on referendum day and something of a carnival atmosphere, helped by the fact that Yes Falkirk had quietly organized a Yes rally at the Kelpies the night before the referendum which attracted hundreds of supporters.[26]

Yes Clackmannanshire was active early in the campaign, with its first stall in Alloa on 4th July 2012, though it had its Yes Scotland formation meeting in Alloa on 1st October. Yes Clackmannanshire had a campaign office in Alloa as well as mini-Yes hub in Clackmannan. The campaign office was initially funded by the SNP but local donations then kept it open, with a crowdfunder late in the campaign to help pay the rent.[27] The Yes group also had its own social media and web page with a film about the group and a small number of blogs by campaigners.[28] Yes campaigning locally was aided by the fact that the SNP had a long-term organisation and presence in the area to act as the basis for campaigning by experienced campaigners (so did Labour locally on behalf of Better Together). It had voter data on party preference and independence support and was able to begin its referendum canvassing well in advance of the launch of Yes Scotland's Yesmo – with Yes canvassing in Menstrie as early as 7th May 2013. Canvassing was a major part of the group's activities, with canvass sessions most nights of the week and sometimes 3-4 a night in different towns and villages in the area as referendum day approached. Whilst Yes Clackmannanshire was the overarching group, other Yes organisations were involved. The Radical Independence Campaign was one of a number of active Yes groups in the area. It took part in a number of canvass events in the area, especially in Alloa. It also campaigned outside the Alloa jobs centre to talk to voters. The Greens were also involved with a Green Yes meeting in Tillycoultry on 12th March 2014. Women for Independence created a local group, that is still active to this day. It took part in the national group's national voter registration day in Alloa on 9th August,[29] held a cocktails and questions night in Alloa on 23rd August 2014 and held a number of pop-up stalls in Alloa to talk with voters. Business for Scotland held a meeting in Alloa to promote independence, whilst there were speaking tour visits by Tommy Sheridan's *Hope over Fear* and the Spirit of Independence campaign bus. The local campaign also created a super Saturday event in Alloa on 13th September 2014 – the last Saturday before the referendum - featuring stalls and campaigning by the Greens, Women for Independence, Business for Scotland, Radical Independence and Farmers for Yes. On referendum day, the different Yes groups ran Gotv activities in the area, with lifts to polling stations as well as a bagpiper leading voters from Harris Court in Alloa to the Bowmar Centre polling station.

Better Together on the Ground

To some extent, Better Together appeared relatively weak on the ground and lacked visibility until comparatively late in the long referendum campaign. However, this appearance was deceptive.

Its activism was less public and therefore less observable and often organized through political parties as part of their normal political campaign activities. For example, local Yes groups were highly public and used social media to promote all their events and activities – in that sense they were an open book in terms of stalls, canvassing and leafleting sessions. Both their supporters and their opponents could see what they were doing and where. Better Together was not like that locally in many areas. It did not promote its activities in the same way but this does not mean it was inactive on the ground it was just quite different to Yes, but through cross-party coordination it moved from parties contacting their own supporters on the independence issue to coordinated campaigning on the ground. Getting it up and running and ensuring competing local parties worked together effectively was the challenge.

Whilst local campaign activity developed, its management by the centre was not straightforward. BT at the centre tried to instigate local activity but lacked the central staff support to run an extensive ground campaign to do so. Unlike the political parties, it had no network of local groups and so had to create one, just like Yes. This situation continued until early 2014 when its campaign support staff expanded in time for the short referendum campaign that began in May 2014. Better Together sought to create national campaign days by posting events on its Nationbuilder website in Glasgow – which meant some events did not really exist as the centre tried to create events online and fill them with local activists later.[30] Some train station leaflet events to catch commuters didn't happen as they were centrally-inspired not least the one for Kirkwall in Orkney which has no train station and no train either (Pike 2015: 83). The community campaign was run by only one staff member – Rob Murray – from the main office in Glasgow and the organization failed to create regional organisers to support the campaign until 2014 (Pike 2015: 83). Local campaigning therefore relied on the parties and the problem of local party co-operation amongst opponents and rivals. BT's local coordinators faced this problem, whilst juggling the demands of their head office to create activists and activism. Weak central support made this difficult though, when the number of campaign staff and regional organisers increased at BT headquarters, it boosted campaign coordination, the appointment of local leaders and activity on the ground as structures, resources and personnel finally came into a positive alignment. Pre-2014, Better Together slowly created local groups and got the political parties to work together on campaigning – often on their own terms not through BT. A logical starting point here for most BT component parties was to contact their own supporters first, via its database and mailing lists. The central organization launched its National Events campaign on its website on 21st August 2012 and this heralded its first national campaign weekend on 25th and 26th August, with stalls and leafleting events up and down Scotland. Regular campaign weekends became a feature of BT's efforts, with leaflet drops organized between the central organisation and local volunteers. Launch events were regularly held for Better Together local groups, and these groups allied with local parties to become mechanisms for activity in terms of leafleting, stalls, phone canvassing and doorstep work. Once the short campaign got underway, new staff and more experienced campaigners were involved in the Better Together ground campaign and activities at all levels increased markedly. Like Yes Scotland it sought to attract and train new volunteers, provide activists support packs, appoint local campaign contacts and create its own volunteers as well as mobilise party activists to work together: none of this was an easy task in a long campaign given divisions between and within the parties. Money spent on the volunteer database in 2012-3 was counter-productive and failed at that time but that on telephone canvassing (Blether Together) as well as doorstep canvassing began to work in 2014,[31] with experienced campaigners at the centre to share the load and manage the campaign more effectively (Pike 2015: 85-6). Structurally, the BT parties may have had an advantage in relation to existing voter data and its connection to voters with telephone landlines and postal votes. The extent of local and national phonebanking, data collection by email and through surveys and mailings plus doorstep canvassing supplemented existing voter data to help the No campaign.

Local campaign activity in the Clackmannanshire, Falkirk and Stirling areas was shared between Better Together and the political parties, mostly meaning Labour and the Conservatives.[32] Labour held all of the local Westminster seats though there was still significant Conservative support and organization in Stirling that was to play a prominent part in the referendum campaign (and filter through to the party's second place performance at the Scottish election in 2016 and to win the Westminster seat in 2017). Stirling is a large constituency of rural areas as well as towns, in which a Conservative vote was evident if not always active. Each of the BT parties had different experiences at the referendum. The campaign re-energised and galvanized Conservative support in the area, so that the party was much stronger after the referendum than before. Its voters were No in 2012 and even stronger No by 18th September. It needed mobilized not convinced. Labour by contrast observed its support moving away, particularly in working class areas as Yes gained support, followed by the convincing SNP election victory in 2015. Its doorstep efforts at the referendum were challenging, especially in areas where the Yes campaign was highly active.

Early meetings between the local Conservative, Labour and Liberal Democrat party organisations cleared the path for effective campaign co-operation throughout the referendum. Better Together stalls were held in the main town centres, though on a much less regular basis than the local Yes groups. However, this did not mean they were not campaigning. They were just campaigning in a different way that was quietly effective through existing political networks and activities. For example, Stirling Labour were active in promoting a No vote at its regular party campaign events through leaflets and canvassing and, specifically campaigning with United with Labour materials as part of a Labour No campaign as early as July 2013, rather than with Better Together material.[33] Labour campaigning at the European election in 2014 involved deploying No messages for the referendum and its student group at Stirling University used Better Together material at fresher's week. Stirling and surrounding areas featured in Jim Murphy's soapbox tour of Scotland – he visited the Raploch Community Centre in Stirling on 19th June 2014 - and the Labour Vote No battle bus visited Stirling on 16th June 2014. Labour activity in both Clackmannanshire and Stirling was aided by the fact that local parties had extensive voter data for these constituencies plus a good organisation (especially in Clackmannanshire), with data collected longer term due to the contested nature of the seats (involving the Conservatives in the case of Stirling and the SNP in the case of Clackmannanshire). This data didn't tell them about voter preferences on independence but did allow them to contact loyal supporters through party appeals and target known supporters and voters.

Both separately and with Labour, the Conservatives were highly active in Stirling throughout the referendum. The national launch of Conservative Friends of the Union in 2012 helped the party and its campaign efforts throughout the referendum. It helped the party to identify and mobilise its support both locally and nationally and provided valuable contacts, some active campaigners and a route to fundraising for the party's campaign. Indeed, it had longer-term effects by mobilizing Conservative support that had lain dormant for some time. Better Together Stirling saw effective campaign coordination and joint working between the Conservatives and Labour and, at times, this exposed the two parties to their different campaign styles: with the more formulaic vote gathering style of Labour canvassers versus the more conversational style of the Conservatives on the doorsteps (Conservatives also saw a shrunken Labour campaign machine on the ground for the first time). Between the two parties and local BT volunteers, most of the homes across Stirling were contacted in person or by telephone. The regular local phone bank sessions were particularly effective as the campaign could rely on party data to guide their phone activities – meaning they were contacting older, long-term and often loyal party supporters – the landline/postal vote electorate - rather than new voters. When that was bolted onto the new data generated by BT, it provided the organization with significant data advantages locally and nationally too. The parties coordinated joint canvassing, leafleting, phoning and letter-writing sessions twice weekly across the Stirling Council area from early January 2014 onwards, with campaign times expanding as the year went on. Demographically, turnout and early voting amongst the Conservative electorate was fairly straightforward to achieve and the strong turnout gave the Tories confidence in the effect of their campaign and the likelihood of a No vote. Getting out the vote in Labour areas was much more problematic with both Labour and Conservative activists focused on ensuring a high turnout in working class areas, running all the way to 9.45 at night on polling day itself.

One thing that the referendum did expose was Labour's weakness on the ground as the party had shrunk in numbers and organizational capacity since 1997. This was apparent in 2014 and even more so in 2015 when Labour in London discovered how little voter identification was in the party's databases for Scottish seats: some had zero contact data (Watson 2015, Cowley and Kavanagh 2016: 90). Labour found itself joined to its Conservative opponents in Better Together due to lack of funds and organization to do much else (Mitchell 2017: 88): providing the reasons for the failure of United with Labour. Half of the party's professional staff in London found themselves diverted into assisting with the referendum in the last months of the campaign and about 100 Labour MPs came North to help. Ed Milliband appeared in Scotland on 10th September as the British party leaders cancelled Prime Minister's question to demonstrate a united position for No just ahead of the vote. However, as Cowley and Kavanagh pointed out, all these staff and MPs should really have been engaged in planning and implementing Labour's 2015 general election campaign instead of being diverted to shore up Labour at the independence referendum (Cowley and Kavanagh 2016: 90).

The Referendum Result and Outcome

The overall result of the referendum saw a No vote of 55.3 per cent as against 44.7 per cent for Yes. Overall 28 local authorities voted No, whilst 4 voted Yes (the latter group involved Dundee, Glasgow, North Lanarkshire and West Dunbartonshire). The local results in central Scotland saw a No vote of 53.8 per cent in Clackmannanshire, 53.5 per cent for No in Falkirk and 59.8 per cent in Stirling. Across Scotland, the highest Yes vote was 57.3 per cent in Dundee and the highest No vote was in Orkney at 67.2 per cent. Of course, within local authorities, there would have been communities (including towns, villages and constituencies) that voted Yes or No, but were included in larger counting areas.

Within the geographical results was a range of demographic factors on the structure of the referendum result.[34] For example, Lord Ashcroft's post-referendum poll of 2,200 voters found slight gender differences in support, with a No-Yes balance of 53-47 per cent amongst men and a No-Yes balance of 56-44 per cent amongst women. In relation to age, the strongest group for No was the over 65s who voted No by 73 to 27 per cent, along with the 55-64 year olds who favoured No by 57 per cent to 43 per cent. However, all other age groups supported Yes, just not in large enough numbers to alter the result. Amongst 16-24 year olds, there was a narrow Yes of 51-49 per cent but 59-41 per cent amongst the 25-34 year olds, 53-47 per cent amongst the 35-44 and 52-48 per cent Yes amongst the 45-54 year olds.[35] When comparing referendum vote to party support at the 2010 UK general election, it was found that 95 per cent of Conservatives voted No, whilst 86 per cent of SNP voters voted Yes. However, of more significance was that 37 per cent of Labour voters and 39 per cent of Liberal Democrats voted Yes: so some party cues had been disrupted during the long campaign.[36] The survey work by the ESRC-funded Scottish Referendum Study was based on a three waves of fieldwork with sample sizes of 4,849 and 3,719, so much more extensive than the Ashcroft survey. The ESRC survey found a gender gap with 56.6 per cent of women voting No but 53.2 per cent of men voting Yes. Voters born in Scotland voted Yes by 52.7 per cent to 47.3 per cent, whereas there was a 72.1 per cent No vote by people born in the rUK and a narrower 57.1 per cent No vote by those born out of the UK. The age demographics were broadly similar to Ashcroft but found smaller gaps amongst older age groups but a very large lead for Yes of 62.5 per cent to 37.5 per cent amongst the 16-19 age group. Simple social class profiles also found 53.6 per cent support for Yes amongst working class voters but 58.3 per cent support for No amongst middle class voters (Henderson and Mitchell 2015).

Conclusion

The longest political campaign in the UK delivered a clear result on the 18th September 2014, on a high turnout of 85 per cent. However, the nature of the result was significant. Whilst Yes clearly lost, it had increased support for independence during the campaign and denied the No campaign a decisive victory of 70-30 per cent: something that would have killed off the independence issue for some time. Perhaps despite itself, Yes had a good campaign and had seen public opinion move in its direction slowly before sliding back in the last week. So, in spite of its defeat, the independence issue lived on after the 18th September in significant ways. Second, No did not mean 'no change' at the referendum. The rapid establishment of the Smith Commission to negotiate increased devolution for the Scottish Parliament brought new powers to devolution.[37] The nature and significance of these new powers was highly contested between the political parties – and still are – but did produce increased powers over income tax, welfare benefits and payments, etc., plus the agreement of a fiscal framework between the Scottish and UK governments (see Cairney 2015; Scotland Act 2016, Tickell 2016). However, neither Smith nor the referendum had solved the Scottish Question and constitutional issues continued to mobilise voters into the 2015 UK election and beyond (with Brexit to do the same after 2016 too, hence debate around a second independence referendum from 2016-17).

Third, who amongst the political parties were the winners and losers of the 2014 referendum as Scottish electoral politics became shaped by the politics of Yes and No? Paradoxically, despite losing the referendum and seeing the resignation of Alex Salmond as First Minister on 19th September, the SNP were post-referendum winners. Not only had the party seen its *raison d'être* centre stage in Scottish and UK politics for 2 years, but its support remained strong during the referendum and its fortunes were transformed by the referendum experience. SNP membership skyrocketed from 19th September 2014 on as it had tens of thousands of new members and profound electoral success at the 2015 UK general election (winning 56 of the 59 Westminster seats in Scotland) (Johns and Mitchell 2016). The momentum from the referendum fed directly into the 2015 general election on the ground (Pringle 2016), with the SNP seeing the highest levels of campaigning and contacts with voters in Britain come the general election (Cowley and Kavanagh 2016: 274). At the same time, both the Scottish Greens and Scottish Socialist Party saw their membership grow significantly. A lot of the political mobilization and campaigning at the referendum found new outlets afterwards. The other winners from the referendum were the Conservatives, who had galvanized their traditional support and also found entry points into the pro-Union electorate, not least in traditional Labour areas. However, this development took time to be observable at the Scottish election in 2016 and the council and Westminster elections of 2017: where the party's strong opposition to a second independence referendum and the Brexit issue brought increased support and seats. The main political casualty of the referendum was the Scottish Labour Party. However it's worth remembering that it had already entered a period of decline that was observable from 2007 onwards due to a variety of factors not simply independence (see Hassan and Shaw 2012). The decline in support was masked by the relatively successful 2010 general election performance, but SNP landslide successes in 2011 and 2015 can now be seen as staging posts on the road to Labour falling to third party status behind the Conservatives in 2016 and 2017 (despite some recovery in seats and votes in 2017).

Endnotes

1. The Scottish Independence Referendum Act 2013.
2. The Scottish Independence Referendum (Franchise) Act 2013.
3. The Scottish Government's initial question was 'Do you agree that Scotland should be an independent country?'
4. Former Labour PM Gordon Brown had apparently favoured a third option on the ballot paper – for a more radical form of devolution – but this was not made public during the referendum though, it was implicit in some of Brown's writing and speeches towards the end of the campaign. See Brown (2017: 402, 408).
5. Before the Vow, Yes had made some inroads into the Labour electorate through campaigning on protecting the NHS.
6. Stephen Noon, 'Yes Campaign Playing the Long Game', *The Scotsman*, 26th January 2014.
7. See tables on Westminster voting intentions 2007-2016 at http://whatscotlandthinks.org/questions/how-would-you-be-likely-to-vote-in-a-uk-general-election#line
8. What Scotland Thinks (2016), Constituency Voting at Scottish Parliament Elections, at http://whatscotlandthinks.org/questions/how-would-you-use-your-constituency-vote-in-a-scottish-parliament-election#line

9.   See tables at http://whatscotlandthinks.org/questions/how-would-you-use-your-constituency-vote-in-a-scottish-parliament-election#line
10.   Though Labour MSP Neil Findlay was concerned at the growth of support for independence amongst Labour voters at this by-election. See Findlay (2017: 38-9).
11.   Employment and unemployment statistics are at https://www.ons.gov.uk/employmentandlabourmarket/peoplenotinwork/unemployment/timeseries/mgsx/lms
12.   Scottish Government (2015), *Regional Employment Patterns in Scotland: Statistics from the Annual Population Survey 2015 publication*, Edinburgh: Scottish Government.
13.   http://webarchive.nationalarchives.gov.uk/20160105160709/http://www.ons.gov.uk/ons/rel/cpi/consumer-price-indices/november-2015/sum-cpi-november-2015.html
14.   Some groups spent so little they didn't need to provide spending returns – such as Yes campaigners Radical Independence, the Spirit of Independence and Wealthy Nation: Electoral Commission (2015), p.40.
15.   Supporters of devo-max were the median voters according to polling at the beginning of 2013. It was the most popular first and second preference of voters. See Liñeira, Henderson and Delaney (2017: 168).
16.   Yes Scotland accounts covered in *Sunday Herald*, 28th August 2016, p.22
17.   This group was important as it could help the Yes campaign to disrupt the use of partisan cues to direct voters to support a party's position at the referendum.
18.   *The Herald*, 30th September 2014.
19.   It didn't help that Yes Scotland's instructions for obtaining signatories to the declaration were vague.
20.   See Better Together leaflets like 'We want the best of both worlds for Scotland' from 2014, *No Thanks* leaflets that promised 'Better Change, Faster Change, Safer Change', billboards stating 'More Job Opportunities & More Powers for Scotland' and lots of messages around 'strength, stability and security'.
21.   Voters would designated as particular 'tribes' within data sets and then targeted with messages see http://www.bbc.co.uk/news/uk-scotland-scotland-politics-23379615
22.   Phone canvassing was a significant part of Better Together's campaign but it was hard to observe. The organization created Blether Together, its own phone canvassing software system for individual phone canvassers but also used collective phonebanking events to gather data and talk to voters. Some of the parties also had their own national and local phone canvassing

activities during the campaign – built upon the fact that they were often calling older, established party supporters with landlines in their homes.

23.   Yes Stirling raised £2,297 for the shop via indiegogo.

24.   Interview with Keith Houston, lead volunteer for Yes Falkirk, 7th September 2016.

25.   The group raised £1,505 to cover the rent of a shop in the town in 2014. See https://www.indiegogo.com/projects/yes-bo-ness-shop

26.   The event is still on you tube at https://www.youtube.com/watch?v=rue22iXaF-k

27.   It raised £1,065 for the campaign office costs - https://www.indiegogo.com/projects/yes-clacks#/

28.   See www.yesclacks.net, with the film on the Wee County Freedom Fighters.

29.   https://www.thunderclap.it/projects/14230-wfi-voter-registration-day

30.   On several occasions SPA archivists turned up at such local BT events to photograph the event for the archive to find no one there or, on one occasion, campaigners arriving after the trains had left.

31.   BT phone canvassing at its Glasgow HQ started as early as 27th March 2013.

32.   In some parts of Scotland such joint campaigning was impossible. In West Lothian for example, the local Labour MSP pulled his campaigners out of a joint canvassing session with the Conservatives in Craigshill in Livingston for fear of the damage it would do (Findlay 2017: 67).

33.   Former Labour PM Gordon Brown had argued for a completely distinctive Labour No campaign as early as 2012, and claimed the support of PM David Cameron and Chancellor George Osborne for this approach but the response from Scottish Labour was weak so a distinctive position was not effectively implemented. See Brown (2017: 402).

34.   For more discussion of these see - http://blog.whatscotlandthinks.org/2014/09/voted-yes-voted/

35.   http://lordashcroftpolls.com/wp-content/uploads/2014/09/Lord-Ashcroft-Polls-Referendum-day-poll-summary-1409191.pdf

36.   http://lordashcroftpolls.com/wp-content/uploads/2014/09/Lord-Ashcroft-Polls-Referendum-day-poll-summary-1409191.pdf

37.   The Smith Commission was complex – it involved negotiations between 5 Holyrood parties and the UK government and parties. Its report is available here, along with some of the post-report changes: http://webarchive.nationalarchives.gov.uk/20151202171017/http://www.smith-commission.scot/

6

Conclusion – Campaigning at Referendums

This book focused on three constitutional referendums held in Scotland between 1979 and 2014. Each was a major national event with a level of political significance that went beyond the referendum itself – meaning it effected post-referendum politics in important ways, with effects on parties, political institutions and policies. These referendums were not containable events but had political spillovers and longer term institutional and political effects for debate, constitutional options and support for political parties. However, one point to make about referendums in Scotland is that they have had a very limited usage. Very few local authorities or governments have chosen to employ the referendum device and, since devolution in 1999, the only official national referendum held was the independence referendum of 2014. It hardly demonstrates an extensive commitment to direct democracy or even to the political use of referendums by political parties and governments at different levels. Even with the large scale engagement and turnout at the 2014 independence referendum, it would be hard to argue that Scotland had anything like a referendum culture. Indeed, in spite of that experience, political decisions remain dominated by orthodox political institutions and decisionmaking. Even with the UK-level Brexit referendum of 23rd June 2016, the referendum device is not notably more popular with the UK government or with its devolved assemblies. Indeed, the Brexit experience might act as a salutory lesson in not using referendums to resolve political problems. These referendums would also count as direct democracy in only a limited definition of the term, given the role of governments in determining the issue and controlling the process.

There is a range of conclusions that can be drawn from this study of three different referendums. Some may be specific to these examples or generalizable to wider referendum experiences. First, referendums definitely present a challenge to campaigners especially in relation to attempts to establish cross-party campaigns. The Electoral Commission's referendum campaign rules in the UK deliberately encourage the formation of umbrella campaign groups for Yes and No propositions. The rules set out processes for applying for designation as lead campaigners, with a set of regulations, requirements and rewards for compliance. In retrospect, it's easy to see how these rules would have brought problems had they been in existence in 1979 – given the level of complexity and conflict inherent in the different Yes campaigns for devolution and, indeed, 1979 provides an ideal example of political divisions preventing the formation of umbrella groups and the determination of some organisations to exist on their own terms – like Labour Vote No.[1] Come 1997, the cross-party situation was much simpler as the pro-change parties came together following early discussions and, under the Scotland Forward umbrella, were determined to avoid the partisan divisions that could damage a Yes vote (remember that was Nigel Smith's fundamental goal in 1996-7). That level of co-operation and avoidance of normal partisan conflict was successful due to political management and agreement at the national and local levels – and its success remains striking given tribal party divisions. The No campaign in 1997 faced no cross-party difficulties at all as it only represented the Conservatives though that party had its own problems at the referendum having lost all of its MPs in Scotland, followed by weakened organization and limited capacity for campaigning come September 1997. The 2014 experience was different to the devolved referendums but had its own challenges. The Better Together trio of Conservatives, Labour and Liberal Democrats had a large amount of government and party support to draw upon, but the political costs of the alliance were obvious for Labour (and partly their own fault for their poor organization in Scotland) and over-identification with the Conservatives and a negative referendum campaign helped feed the party's precipitous decline at the 2015 UK general election (foreshadowed by seat losses to the SNP in the 2007 and 2011 Scottish elections). The Better Together coalition experienced a lot of internal conflict during its existence, though most of it was from friendly fire. Moreover, despite all the organisational difficulties, it won the referendum convincingly. Yes Scotland, also faced considerable internal difficulties and, in terms of its composition, was lop-sided due to the size (and extensive experience) of the SNP compared to the Greens and Scottish Socialist Party. There was no escaping this throughout the campaign as the SNP brought most expertise, staff, resources and finance to the Yes campaign, compared to the more modest experiences of the other parties. Despite its flaws, though, the cross-party aspect of Yes Scotland was reasonably effective, especially when tied to the development of a large grassroots campaign. For the Electoral Commission, there was also the difficulty of regulating so many different organisations for Yes and No that were not part of the official umbrella groups but independent of them – with debate around the issue of joint working (Electoral Commission 2015), with some Electoral Commission investigation into the issue.[2]

The second conclusion that can be made is that campaigns matter at referendums, albeit in different ways. For example, a series of poor Yes campaigns in 1979, allied to political conflicts and a highly negative economic environment, helped to change healthy opinion poll leads for a Scottish Assembly to dead even opinion polls come 1st March (Macartney 1981: 32). The efforts of both Yes and No contributed to a very mixed result at this referendum, though the rules made it a definite No as 40 per cent of the electorate had not voted for devolution. The next devolution campaign from 1996-7 was also one in which the campaign mattered - in the sense that the Yes campaign undertook considerable preparation and a set of charm offensives with the political parties to ensure a positive, unified campaign. The intention here was to 'maintain' existing support for a devolved parliament and to ensure that these supporters actually turned out, through mobilising campaign efforts, use of the Scotland Forward declaration and the types of 'balloon' campaigning mentioned in chapter 4. Scotland Forward and the parties sought a careful, united campaign, whilst the No campaign barely got out of the starting blocks to organize in 1997. In 2014 the campaign also mattered as opinion changed significantly both on the binary issue of independence itself but also on specific issues within the campaign like currency sharing (McEwen and Keating 2017: 194). Why it changed is open to speculation. Was it the ground campaign, the air war, TV debates, voter reactions to negative or positive campaigning or something more prosaic?

Third, negative campaigning was utilized at all three referendums, with varying degrees of success. For example, Jim Sillars referred to the No campaign in 1979 as the original Project Fear – with media against devolution and big business playing some of the same tunes as in 2013-14 over the economy, borders, the BBC and all sorts of other topics (Sillars 2015: 3-4). In some ways, the No campaign of 1979 was actually running an anti-independence campaign, cleverly conflating devolution and independence to boost the No vote and win support by over-identification of a Scottish Assembly with the SNP (which was campaigning for devolution at the time). Similar negative themes were adopted by Think Twice (or pay the price) in 1997, as it focused on the economy, the cost of the new institution, paying for new politicians instead of public services as well as a specific focus on the taxation power proposed for the new parliament (which was viewed as a political problem by Labour, hence the decision to have a second referendum question on tax-varying powers). Negative campaigning was also a prominent feature of the independence referendum. Better Together did not disappoint in dubbing itself Project Fear though, as the No campaign, it was to be expected to use negative arguments against change, especially as it was aiming at ensuring undecideds did not vote for independence. Picking material themes around economic security – during a period of economic turbulence following the Great Financial Crisis - was unsurprising especially as it could ask all sorts of questions about the uncertain future and present a negative prospectus for Scotland. It was not alone in using some negative campaigning, Yes Scotland did it too, over the UK threat to the Scottish NHS in the last months of the campaign, as well as prospect of a future Conservative government at the general election scheduled for 7th May 2015.

Fourth, partisan cues were important at all three referendums and parties and umbrella groups understood their importance. In 1997, Scotland Forward's whole strategy was based around maintaining the coherence of party cues at the referendum – it wanted unity within and between Labour, the Liberal Democrats and the SNP to ensure a common, positive message. Scotland Forward wanted to prevent a party like Labour from fragmenting into Yes and No camps like in 1979 – when the emergence and activism of Labour Vote No was important and damaged the case for devolution. In 2014, some of Yes Scotland's efforts were directed at publicizing the extent of Labour support for independence using political figures and messaging to disrupt Labour's partisan cues. The campaign group Labour for Independence assisted this, but was too small to significantly alter the result, even though it helped to detach Labour voters from No to Yes. What Yes Scotland actually needed here was sitting Labour MSPs or former First Ministers to come out publically for Yes to give this part of the campaign more impetus. Contrast this situation with the Brexit referendums scenario in which the Conservatives were publicly divided for Leave and Remain at all levels – cabinet, parliament, councils, members – and in which prominent Labour MPs came out for Leave, and you get the sense in which Labour for Independence underperformed in 2014.

Fifth, local campaigning was a feature of all three referendums and especially so with the 2014 independence referendum. Here, we probably saw the largest and longest ground campaign in Scottish and UK politics. In 1979 and 1997 the political parties were most the prominent referendum actors by some distance, with business, trade union and civic groups also involved, whereas in 2014, the scope of political actors was much broader. This reality was evident in the nature of the organizational returns for the referendum – the extent of groups who had to register and declare their spending – but also in the level of campaign organisations across the referendum. Significantly, many of these campaigns operated at both the national and local level and sought to take their message to the public directly through stalls, leaflets, talks, doorstep canvassing and a variety of other methods. Local grassroots activity was a key aspect of the work of both the Yes and No campaigns in 2014, but did it actually work? Yes Scotland arguably had the larger ground campaign in 2014, but did it work? It certainly contributed to increasing the size of the Yes vote but that contribution did not lead Yes to win. The local ground wars evident in Clackmannanshire, Falkirk and Stirling were impressive – and probably some of the largest popular mobilisations these areas will ever seen, but the No vote won in each area.

Significantly, the role of Yes volunteers was measured in Iain Black and Sara Marsden's (2016) online survey of activists following the conclusion of the independence referendum. Black and Marsden conducted an online survey of 64 questions to tap levels of activism, the social background of volunteers, ideological leanings, engagement in different types of Yes groups, etc. The survey results need to be treated with caution because they involved a self-selecting group of activists, contacted via Yes social media following on from the referendum itself: so, they don't offer up a picture of volunteer activism and engagement as a whole though the study had a good sample size of 993 volunteers. The study found volunteers tended to be male, middle aged, highly educated and from higher socio-economic groups (Black and Marsden 2016: 4-5), and 44 per cent were established members of a political party before the referendum campaign had concluded (Black and Marsden 2016: 6), with many others joining parties late on in the referendum campaign or in the immediate aftermath. Whilst many of the volunteers were new to political campaigning, many were members of a range of organisations like trade unions, professional associations, charity and peace groups, youth groups, womens' groups, etc. (Black and Marsden 2016: 24), so there was a lot of political experience and involvement amongst the volunteers from other areas of civic life.

Volunteers became active in waves throughout the campaign and 71.8 per cent were active in their local Yes group, with 39.2 per cent involved with Radical Independence, 30.8 per cent with National Collective and 23.8 per cent with Business for Scotland. Amongst women survey respondents, 67.7 per cent of volunteers were active with Women for Independence (Black and Marsden 2016: 7). Black and Marsden's study also asked volunteers to state their most frequent activities at the referendum as well as their least frequent. The most frequent activities by Yes volunteers were political conversations with family, friends and the public, online discussions, wearing Yes merchandise and displaying posters, leafleting, attending public meetings and canvassing (Black and Marsden 2016: 8). Volunteers funded their local Yes group as well as donating to Yes Scotland (Black and Marsden 2016: 30) and 25.4 per cent of them took part in doorstep canvassing very frequently, with 17.3 per cent taking part frequently and 19.1 per cent occasionally (Black and Marsden 2016: 30): so there was quite a lot of structured voter engagement, with voter registration also a feature of volunteer activity, with 8.3 per cent undertaking registration very frequently and 12.4 per cent frequently (Ibid: 30). Amongst the least popular activities was telephone canvassing, managing online groups, designing local campaign materials etc. (Black and Marsden 2016: 8). Though, significantly, these still involved large numbers of people. In addition, volunteering also involved considerable time commitments by campaigners, with 48.6 per cent of respondents stating they spent 1-5 hours a week on the Yes campaign and a further 25.1 per cent reporting they spent 6-10 hours a week. Smaller numbers of volunteers reported much higher levels of time on the campaign, with some active for over 40 hours a week (Black and Marsden 2016: 7).

Sixth, when it comes to campaigning models and change we can see a broad transition across Farrell and Webb's three periods of campaigning. By the independence referendum of course, the internet and social media were much more important though again, even then, they were probably underplayed somewhat compared to the 2015 UK general election and the Brexit referendum of 2016. There were several reasons for this not least that Facebook and Twitter were still relatively new and growing amongst the public from 2012-14 and were not so effective as campaigning platforms as they were to become. Campaigners utilized emails, campaign platforms like Nationbuilder and social media to promote their message, advertise events, sign up supporters and build popular networks for their campaigns nationally and locally, but the spend on some of these areas appears limited (indeed the attraction of some platforms was that they were free or relatively cheap). The fact that so many activists and supporters were sharing online content for free during the referendum meant that paid reach was less important but even so, comparing the spending on Facebook of Better Together and Yes in 2014 as against Leave in 2016 is striking: financially these are worlds apart.

Finally, consider the aftershocks of the referendums, especially from 2014. Each referendum had some political ramifications and effects on political life long after the referendum was held – what they did to the constitutional question in terms of the constitutional debate, institutions and policy as well as to the fortunes of the political parties. Furthermore, in 2014, the construction of a campaign infrastructure fed into considerable political success for the SNP after the referendum as so many Yes campaigners joined the party from 19th September onwards, providing a surge of new members, money and campaigning efforts into the party. This was part of the reason for the SNP's astonishing success in 2015 – a new active grassroots across all Scottish constituencies – but the referendum also created a continuing and active Yes movement. National Collective may have disbanded following the referendum, but Business for Scotland, the Radical Independence Campaign, Women for Independence, the Common Weal all grew, whilst individual Yes groups became more permanent and incorporated into the new National Yes Registry. On the other side of the independence debate, the Conservatives grew during the referendum in terms of campaigning and electoral success and the pro-Union Scotland in Union group was created to act as a nascent Better Together campaign too. So, in short, the aftershocks of the referendum continued into politics and organizational development long after 10pm on 18th September 2014. And some of them, like some of the organizations discussed here, will play some role in any future referendum on the independence question.

Endnotes

1.   Arguably, such rules might well have pushed the different Yes campaigns together into one, uneasy umbrella organization, but that's difficult to say.
2.   http://www.heraldscotland.com/news/13872800.Elections_watchdog_finds_no_evidence_of_unlawful_joint_working_between_SNP_and_BFS/

Bibliography

Adamson, Kevin and Peter Lynch (2014) (Eds), *Scottish Political Parties and the 2014 Independence Referendum*, Cardiff: Welsh Academic Press.

Altman, David (2014), *Direct Democracy Worldwide*, Cambridge: Cambridge University Press.

Ascherson, Neil (2002), *Stone Voices: The Search for Scotland*, London: Granta.

Baimbridge, Mark (2007), 'The Pre-History of the Referendum', in Mark Baimbridge (Ed), *The 1975 Referendum on Europe: Volume 1, Reflections of the Participants*, Exeter: Imprint Academic.

Bale, Tim and Paul Webb (2015), 'Grunts in the ground game: UK party members in the 2015 general election', Paper prepared for the Conference on 'The 2015 British General Election: Parties, Politics, and the Future of the United Kingdom', 2 September 2015, UC Berkeley.

Barr, Andrew Redmond (2016), *The Summer of Independence: Stories from a Nation in the Making*, Edinburgh: Word Power.

Bennett, Owen (2016), *The Brexit Club*, London: Biteback.

Better Together (2014), *Local Leaders Handbook*, Glasgow: Better Together.

Black, Iain and Sara Marsden (2016), *The Yes volunteers: Capturing the 'Biggest grassroots campaign in Scotland's History'*, Glasgow, Common Weal.

Blain, Neil and David Hutchison (2016) (Eds), *Scotland's Referendum and the Media: National and International Perspectives*, Edinburgh: Edinburgh University Press.

Blair, Tony (2010), *A Journey*, London: Random House.

Bochel, John, David Denver and Allan Macartney (1981) (Eds), *The Referendum Experience: Scotland 1979*, Aberdeen: Aberdeen University Press.

Bogdanor, Vernon (1996), *Politics and the Constitution*, Aldershot: Dartmouth

Bogdanor, Vernon (1994), 'Western Europe', in David Butler and Austin Ranney (Eds), *Referendums around the world*, London: Macmillan.

Bogdanor, Vernon (1979), article from the Spectator magazine, 10th March 1979, reprinted in Lindsay Paterson (1998), *A Diverse Assembly*, Edinburgh: Edinburgh University Press, p. 132.

Bremner, Stewart (2015), *The Early Days of a Better Nation*, Edinburgh: Imagined Images Editions.

Brown, Gordon (2017), *My Life, Our Times*, London: Bodley Head.

Brown, Gordon (2014), *My Scotland, Our Britain: A Future Worth Sharing*, London: Simon and Schuster.

Büchi, Rolf (2011), 'Local Popular Votes in Finland – procedures and experiences', in Theo Schiller (Ed), *Local Direct Democracy in Europe*, Wiesbaden: VS Verlag.

Butler, David and Austin Ranney (1994) (Eds), *Referendums around the world*, London: Macmillan.

Butler, David and Uwe Kitzinger (1976), *The 1975 Referendum*, London: Macmillan.

Cairney, Paul (2015), 'The Scottish Independence Referendum: What are the Implications of a No Vote?', *Political Quarterly*, Vol. 85, issue 2, pp.186-191.

Canavan, Dennis (2009), *Let the People Decide*, Edinburgh: Birlinn.

Carman, Christopher, Robert Johns and James Mitchell (2014), *More Scottish than British: The 2011 Scottish Parliament Election*, London: Palgrave.

Clarke, Harold, Matthew Goodwin and Paul Whiteley (2017), 'Why Britain Voted for Brexit: An Individual-Level Analysis of the 2016 Referendum Vote', *Parliamentary Affairs*, Volume 70, Issue 3, pp. 439–464.

Clarke, Harold, Matthew Goodwin and Paul Whiteley (2017a), *Brexit: Why Britain Voted to Leave the European Union*, Cambridge: Cambridge University Press.

Cochrane, Alan (2014), *Alex Salmond: My Part in his Downfall*, London: Biteback.

Cooper, Andrew (2016), 'The Conservative Campaign', in Dominic Wring, Roger Mortimore and Simon Atkinson (Eds), *Political Communication in Britain: Polling, Campaigning and Media in the 2015 General Election*, London: Palgrave Macmillan.

Conservative Party (2015), *Strong leadership, A Clear Economic Plan, A Brighter, More Secure Future*, London: Conservative Party

Cowley, Phillip and Dennis Kavanagh (2016), *The British General Election of 2015*, London: Palgrave Macmillan.

Curtice, John (2013), 'Politicians, voters and democracy: The 2011 UK Referendum on the Alternative Vote', *Electoral Studies*, 32, pp.215-223.

Dalyell, Tam (2011), *The Importance of Being Awkward*, Edinburgh: Birlinn.

Dalyell, Tam, Archive, Acc. 12918, National Library of Scotland, box 18.

Department for Transport (2015), *The Northern Powerhouse: One Agenda, One Economy, One North*, London: HMSO.

Denver, David and Gordon Hands (2006), 'Post-Fordism in the Constituencies? The Continuing Development of Constituency Campaigning in Britain', in David Farrell and Rudiger Schmitt-Beck (Eds), *Do Political Campaigns Matter? Campaign Effects in Elections and Referendums*, London: Routledge.

Denver, David, Gordon Hands and Iain MacAllister (2004), 'The Electoral Impact of Constituency Campaigning in Britain, 1992-2001', *Political Studies*, Vol. 52, issue 2, pp.289-306.

Denver, David, James Mitchell, Charles Pattie and Hugh Bochel (2000), *Scotland Decides: the Devolution issue and the 1997 referendum*, London: Routledge.

Denver, David and Gordon Hands (1997), *Modern Constituency Electioneering*, London: Frank Cass.

Dommett, Ian and Iain Black (2016), '11 lessons the Yes campaign must learn to win a second referendum', *The National*, 6th August 2016.

Electoral Commission (2017), *Report on the Regulation of campaigners at the referendum on the UK's membership of the European Union held on 23 June 2016*, London: Electoral Commission.

Electoral Commission (2016), *The 2016 EU Referendum: Report on the 23 June 2016 referendum on the UK's membership of the European Union*, London: Electoral Commission.

Electoral Commission (2016), *UK Parliamentary General Election 2015: Campaign spending report*, London: Electoral Commission.

Electoral Commission (2015), *Scottish Independence Referendum: Report on the regulation of campaigners at the independence referendum held on 18 September 2014*, London: Electoral Commission.

Electoral Commission (2014), *Scottish Independence Referendum: Report on the referendum held on 18th September 2014*, London: Electoral Commission.

Electoral Commission (2011a), *Referendum on the voting system for UK parliamentary elections*, London: Electoral Commission.

Electoral Commission (2011), *Report on the referendum on law-making powers of the national Assembly for Wales*, London: Electoral Commission.

Electoral Commission (2005), *The 2004 North East regional assembly and local government referendums*, London: Electoral Commission.

Electoral Reform Society (2016), *It's Good to Talk: Doing referendums differently after the EU Vote*, London: Electoral Reform Society.

Farrell, David and Paul Webb (2002), Political Parties as Campaign Organizations' unpublished paper at http://geser.net/par/farrell_webb.pdf.

Farrell, David and Paul Webb (1998), 'Political Parties as Campaign Organizations', paper presented to project meeting on 'Unthinkable Democracy', University of California's Centre for the Study of Democracy, 1st to 4th March 1998.

159

Farrell, David and Rüdiger Schmitt-Beck (2002) (Eds), *Do Political Campaigns Matter? Campaign Effects in Elections and Referendums*, London: Routledge.

Findlay, Neil (2017), *Socialism and Hope; a journey through turbulent times*, Edinburgh: Luath.

Fisher, Justin (2015), 'Party Finance: The Death of the National Campaign', *Parliamentary Affairs*, 68, pp.133-153.

Fisher, Justin, Edward Fieldhouse and David Cutts (2014), 'Members are not the only fruit: Volunteer Activity in British Political Parties at the 2010 General Election', *British Journal of Politics and International Relations*, Vol. 16, pp.75-95

Fisher, Justin, Ron Johnston, David Cutts, Charles Pattie and Edward Fieldhouse (2014), 'You Get What You (don't) Pay for: The Impact of Volunteer Labour and Candidate Spending at the 2010 British General Election', *Parliamentary Affairs*, vol.67, pp.804-824.

Fisher, Justin, David Cutts and Edward Fieldhouse (2011), 'The electoral effectiveness of constituency campaigning in the 2010 British general election: The 'triumph' of Labour?', *Electoral Studies*, Vol.30, no,4, pp.816-828.

Fisher, J. and Denver, D. (2008) 'From Foot-Slogging to Call Centres and Direct Mail: A Framework for Analysing the Development of District-Level Campaigning', *European Journal of Political Research*, 47, pp. 794–826.

Fowler, John (1981), 'Broadcasting', in John Bochel, David Denver and Allan Macartney (Eds), *The Referendum Experience: Scotland 1979*, Aberdeen: Aberdeen University Press.

Franklin, Bob (2004), *Packaging Politics: Political Communications in Britain's Media Democracy*, London: Bloomsbury Academic.

Geoghegan, Peter (2015), *The People's Referendum: Why Scotland Will Never Be The Same Again*, Edinburgh: Luath Press.

Gould, Philip (1998), *The Unfinished Revolution: How New Labour Changed British Politics Forever*, London: Little Brown and Company.

Harvey, Malcolm (2014), 'The Scottish Liberal Democrats and the 2014 Independence Referendum', in Kevin Adamson and Peter Lynch (Eds), *Scottish Political Parties and the 2014 Independence Referendum*, Cardiff: Welsh Academic Press.

Hassan, Gerry and Eric Shaw (2012), *The Strange Death of Labour Scotland*, Edinburgh: Edinburgh University Press.

Hassan, Gerry and Peter Lynch (2011), *The Almanac of Scottish Politics*, London: Politicos.

Henderson, Ailsa and James Mitchell (2015), *The Scottish Question Six Months On*, Transatlantic Seminar Series, 27th March 2015.

Johns, Rob and James Mitchell (2016), *Takeover: Explaining the Extraordinary Rise of the SNP*, London: Biteback.

Johnston, Ron and Charles Pattie (2014), *Money and Electoral Politics*, Cambridge: Polity Press.

Johnston, Ron, David Cutts, Charles Pattie and Justin Fisher (2012), 'We've got them on a list: contacting, canvassing and voting in a British general election campaign', *Electoral Studies*, 31, pp.317-329.

Keating, Michael (2017) (Ed), *Debating Scotland: Issues of Independence and Union at the 2014 Referendum*, Oxford: Oxford University Press.

Kellas, James (1989), *The Scottish Political System*, Cambridge: Cambridge University Press.

Kemp, Arnold (1993), *The Hollow Drum: Scotland Since the War*, Edinburgh: Mainstream.

Knock, Katy (2006), 'The North East Referendum: Lesson Learnt?', *Parliamentary Affairs*, Vol. 59, no.4, pp.682-693.

Kobach, Kris (1994), 'Switzerland' in David Butler and Austin Ranney (Eds), *Referendums around the world*, London: Macmillan.

Lecca, Patrizio, Peter McGregor and J. Kim Swales (2017), 'Economy', in Michael Keating (Ed), *Debating Scotland: Issues of Independence and Union in the 2014 Referendum*, Oxford: Oxford University Press.

LeDuc, Lawrence (2007), 'Opinion Formation and Change in Referendum Campaigns', in Claes de Vreese (ed), *The Dynamics of Referendum Campaigns: An International Perspective*, London: Macmillan.

LeDuc, Laurence (2003), *The Politics of Direct Democracy: referendums in global perspective*, Peterborough: Broadview Press.

LeDuc, Lawrence (2002), 'Referendums and Elections: how do campaigns differ?', in David Farrell and Rüdiger Schmitt-Beck (2002) (eds), *Do Political Campaigns Matter? Campaign Effects in Elections and Referendums*, London: Routledge.

Lees-Marshment, Jennifer (2014), *Political Marketing: Principles and Applications*, London: Routledge.

Liñeira, Robert, Ailsa Henderson and Liam Delaney (2017), 'Voters' Response to the Campaign: Evidence from the Survey', in Michael Keating (Ed), *Debating Scotland: Issues of Independence and Union in the 2014 Referendum*, Oxford: Oxford University Press.

Liñera, Robert and Daniel Cetra (2015), 'The Independence Case in Comparative Perspective', *The Political Quarterly*, Vol. 88, pp.257–264.

Lijphart, Arend (1984), *Democracies: Patterns of Majoritarian and Consensus Government in Twenty-One Countries*, London: Yale University Press.

Macartney, Allan (1981), 'The Protagonists', in John Bochel, David Denver and Allan Macartney (Eds), *The Referendum Experience: Scotland 1979*, Aberdeen: Aberdeen University Press.

McAlpine, Robin (2016), *Determination: how Scotland can become independent by 2021*, Glasgow: Common Weal.

McHarg, Aileen, Tom Mullen, Alan Page and Neil Walker (2016) (Eds), *The Scottish Independence Referendum: Constitutional and Political Implications*, Oxford: Oxford University Press.

McLean, Bob (2005), *Getting it Together: The History of the Campaign for a Scottish assembly/Parliament 1980-1999*, Edinburgh: Luath Press.

McLetchie, David and Michael Forsyth (1975), *The Scottish Conservative Party: A New Model for a New Dimension*, Federation of Conservative Students.

MacWhirter, Iain (2014), *Disunited Kingdom: How Westminster Won A Referendum But Lost Scotland*, Glasgow: Cargo.

MacWhirter, Iain (2013), *Road to Referendum*, Glasgow: Cargo.

Mitchell, James (2016), 'The Referendum Campaign', in Aileen McHarg, Tom Mullen, Alan Page and Neil Walker (Eds), *The Scottish Independence Referendum*, Oxford: Oxford University Press.

Mitchell, James, Lynn Bennie and Rob Johns (2012), *The Scottish National Party: Transition to Power*, Oxford: Oxford University Press.

Mitchell, James (1996), *Strategies for Self-government*, Edinburgh: Polygon.

Mitchell, James (1990), *Conservatives and the Union*, Edinburgh: Edinburgh University Press.

Moore, Martin (2016), 'Facebook, the Conservatives and the Risk to Fair and Open Elections in the UK', *Political Quarterly*, July–September, Volume 87, Issue 3, pp.424-30.

Mullen, Andy (2007), From Imperial Third Force to the 1975 Referendum', in Mark Baimbridge (Ed), *The 1975 Referendum on Europe: Volume 1, Reflections of the Participants*, Exeter: Imprint Academic.

Noon, Stephen (2014), *Building a Groundswell for Yes*, National Collective, 8th April 2013.

Norris, Pippa (2000), *A Virtuous Circle: Political Communications in Post-industrial Societies*, Cambridge University Press.

Norris, Pippa (1997), *Electoral Change Since 1945*, Oxford: Blackwell.

Oliver, Craig (2017), *Unleashing Demons: The Inside Story of Brexit*, London: Hodder.

Paterson, Lindsay (1998) (Ed), *A Diverse Assembly: Debate on a Scottish Parliament*, Edinburgh: Edinburgh University Press.

Pattie, Charles and Ron Johnston (2009), 'Still Talking, But is Anyone Listening?', *Party Politics*, Vol.15, No.4, pp.411-434.

Pattie, Charles, David Denver, James Mitchell and Hugh Bochel (1999), 'Partisanship, national identity and constitutional preferences: an exploration of voting in the Scottish devolution referendum of 1997', *Electoral Studies*, Volume 18, No.3, pp. 305-322.

Pike, Joe (2015), *Project Fear*, London: Biteback.

Plasser, Fritz (2002), *Global Political Campaigning*, London: Praeger.

Pringle, Kevin (2016), 'The SNP Campaign', in Dominic Wring, Roger Mortimore and Simon Atkinson (Eds), *Political Communication in Britain: Polling, Campaigning and Media in the 2015 General Election*, London: Palgrave Macmillan.

Qvortrup, Matt (2014), 'Referendums and Sovereignty', in Kevin Adamson and Peter Lynch (Eds), *Scottish Political Parties and the 2014 Independence Referendum*, Cardiff: Welsh Academic Press.

Qvortrup, Matt (2014) (Ed), *Referendums Around the World: The Continued Growth of Direct Democracy*, London: Palgrave Macmillan.

Qvortrup (2013), *Direct democracy: A comparative study of the theory and practice of government by the people*, Manchester: Manchester University Press.

Qvortrup, Matt (2012), 'Voting on Electoral Reform: A Comparative Perspective on the Alternative Vote Referendum in the United Kingdom', *The Political Quarterly*, Vol.83, No.1, January-March, pp.108-116.

Qvortrup, Matt (2007), *The Politics of Participation: From Athens to E-Democracy*, Manchester: Manchester University Press.

Qvortrup (2005), *A comparative study of referendums: Government by the people*, Manchester: Manchester University Press.

Quinlan, Stephen, Mark Shephard and Lindsay Paterson (2015), 'Online discussion and the 2014 Scottish Independence referendum: flaming keyboards or forums of deliberation', *Electoral Studies*, Vol. 38, pp. 192–205.

Rallings, Colin, Michael Thrasher and David Cowling (2014), 'Mayoral referendums and elections revisited', *British Politics*, Vol.9, 1, pp.2-28.

Rallings, Colin, Michael Thrasher, Galina Borisyuk (2013), 'Local campaign activity and voting', *Electoral Studies*, 32, pp.285-293,

Rallings, Colin and Michael Thrasher (2006), 'Just Another Expensive Talking Shop: Public Attitudes and the 2004 Regional Assembly in the North East of England', *Regional Studies*, Vol.40.8, pp.927-936.

Reilly, Shauna and Ryan Yonk (2015), *Direct Democracy in the United States: Petitioners as a Reflection of Society*, London: Routledge.

Reilly, Shauna (2010), *Design, Meaning and Choice in Direct Democracy: The Influences of Petitioners and Voters*, London: Routledge.

Riddoch, Lesley (2015), *Wee White Blossom*, Edinburgh: Luath Press.

Ross, Tim and Tom McTague (2017), *Betting the House: The Inside Story of the 2017 Election*, London: Biteback.

Salmond, Alex (2015), *The Dream Shall Never Die: 100 Days That Changed Scotland Forever*, London: William Collins.

Scammell, Margaret (2014), *Consumer Democracy*, Cambridge: Cambridge University Press.

Scammell, Margaret (1995), *Designer Politics: How Elections Are Won*, London: Macmillan.

Schmitt-Beck, Rüdiger and David Farrell (2002), 'Studying Political Campaigns and their effects', in David Farrell and Rüdiger Schmitt-Beck (2002) (eds), *Do Political Campaigns Matter? Campaign Effects in Elections and Referendums*, London: Routledge.

Schiller, Theo (2011) 'Local Direct Democracy in Europe – a comparative Overview', in Theo Schiller (Ed), *Local Direct Democracy in Europe*, Wiesbaden: VS Verlag.

Scotland Act 2016 (2016), London: The Stationary Office.

Scotland is British (1978), *The Scotland is British Campaign Answers Seven Questions Vital To Your Future*, Glasgow: Scotland is British.

Scottish Conservative Party (2014), *Commission on the Future Governance of Scotland*, Edinburgh: Scottish Conservatives.

Scottish Constitutional Convention (1995), *Scotland's Parliament*, Edinburgh: Scottish Constitutional Convention.

Scottish Government (2016), *Scottish Independence Referendum bill (consultation draft)*, Edinburgh: Scottish Government.

Scottish Government (2015), *Scottish Elections (Reduction of Voting Age) Act*, *Edinburgh*: Scottish Government.

Scottish Government (2012), *Agreement between the United Kingdom Government and the Scottish Government on a referendum on independence for Scotland*, Edinburgh: Scottish Government.

Scottish Government (2007), *Scottish Economic Statistics 2007*, Edinburgh: Scottish Government.

Scottish Labour Party (2014), *Together We Can – Grow, Care, Achieve, Prosper, Succeed*, Glasgow: United with Labour.

Scottish Labour Devolution Commission (2014), *Powers for a purpose - Strengthening Accountability and Empowering People*, Glasgow: Scottish Labour Party.

Scottish Labour Party (1997), *Scottish Labour Party Referendum Campaign Pack, 11th September 1997*, Glasgow: Scottish Labour.

Scottish Liberal Democrats (2014), *Campbell II - The second report of the Home Rule and Community Rule Commission*, Edinburgh: Scottish Liberal Democrats.

Scottish Liberal Democrats (2012), *Federalism – the Best Future for Scotland*, The Home Rule and Community Commission of the Scottish Liberal Democrats. Edinburgh: Scottish Liberal Democrats.

Scottish National Party (2016), *Re-elect* Manifesto, Edinburgh: SNP.

Seyd, Patrick and Paul Whiteley (1992), *Labour's Grassroots: The Politics of Party Membership*, London: Clarendon.

Shaw, Eric (2014), 'The Scottish Labour Party and the Independence Referendum', in Kevin Adamson and Peter Lynch (Eds), *Scottish Political Parties and the 2014 Independence Referendum*, Cardiff: Welsh Academic Press.

Shipman, Tim (2016), *All Out War*, London: William Collins.

Shorthouse, Robert (2015), *Key Take Aways from Scotland's Better Together Campaign*, presentation to Campaigning Summit, Vienna at https://www.youtube.com/watch?v=W0PqSQ5izOQ

Sillars, Jim (2015) *In Place of Failure: Making it Yes Next Time*, Glasgow: Vagabond Voices.

Sillars, Jim (2014), *In Place of Fear II: A Socialist Programme for an Independent Scotland*, Glasgow: Vagabond Voices.

Sillars, Jim (1995), *Scotland – The Case for Optimism*, Edinburgh: Polygon.

Smith, Alex (2011), *Devolution and the Scottish Conservatives: Banal Activism, Electioneering and the Politics of Irrelevance*, Manchester: Manchester University Press.

Stirling Branch SNP (1978), Minutes of Stirling SNP Branch, 14th December 1978.

Sullivan, Willie (2014), *The Missing Scotland*, Edinburgh: Luath Press.

Swan, Coree Brown and Bettina Petersohn (2017), 'The Currency Issue: Contested Narratives on Currency Union and Independence', in Michael Keating (Ed), *Debating Scotland: Issues of Independence and Union in the 2014 Referendum*, Oxford: Oxford University Press.

Tickell, Andrew (2016), 'The Technical Jekyll and the Political Hyde', in Aileen McHarg, Tom Mullen, Alan Page and Neil Walker (Eds), *The Scottish Independence Referendum*, Oxford: Oxford University Press.

Torrance, David (2014), 'The Scottish Conservatives and the 2014 Independence Referendum', in Kevin Adamson and Peter Lynch (Eds), *Scottish Political Parties and the 2014 Independence Referendum*, Cardiff: Welsh Academic Press.

Torrance, David (2014), *100 Days of Hope and Fear: How Scotland's Referendum was Lost and Won*, Edinburgh: Luath Press.

Torrance, David (2013), *The Battle for Britain*, London: Biteback.

Torrance, David (2010), *Salmond: Against the Odds*, Edinburgh: Birlinn.

Torrance, David (2009), *We in Scotland: Thatcherism in a Cold Climate*, Edinburgh: Birlinn.

Vreese, Claes de (2007), 'Context, Elites, Media and Public Opinion in Referendums: When Campaigns Really Matter', in Claes de Vreese (ed), *The Dynamics of Referendum Campaigns: An International Perspective*, London: Macmillan.

Watson, Iain (2015), *Five million Conversations: How Labour Lost an Election and Rediscovered its Grassroots*, Edinburgh: Luath Press.

Whiteley, Paul, Patrick Seyd and Antony Billinghurst (2006) *Third force politics: Liberal Democrats at the grassroots*. Oxford: Oxford University Press.

Whiteley, Paul and Pat Seyd (2003), 'How to win a landslide by really trying: the effects of local campaigning on voting in the 1997 British general election', *Electoral Studies* 22, 301-24.

Whiteley, Paul, Patrick Seyd and Jeremy Richardson (1994), *True Blues: The Politics of Conservative Party Membership*, Oxford: Oxford University Press.

Wilson, Gordon (2009), *SNP: The Turbulent Years 1960-1990*, Stirling: Scots Independent Publishing.

Wyn Jones. Richard and Roger Scully (2012), *Wales Says Yes*, Cardiff: University of Wales Press.

Yes Falkirk (2013), *Scotland 2014*, Glasgow: Yes Scotland.

Yes Stirling (2013), *Yes Stirling Newsletter*, April, 2013.

welsh academic press

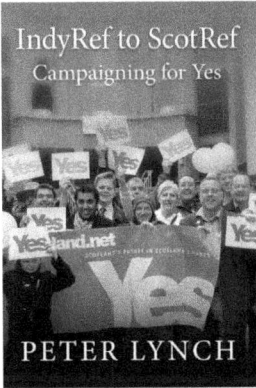

IndyRef to ScotRef
Campaigning for Yes

Peter Lynch

'Peter Lynch captures perfectly the real Yes campaign, not the one fought in TV studios or parliaments but on the ground, across every street in Scotland.'
Ross Greer MSP, Yes Scotland Communities Coordinator 2012-14

'IndyRef to ScotRef is a brilliant and insightful account of what powered the Yes movement from the perspective of an activist, and perfectly describes the shared experiences of many dedicated people and groups across Scotland who contributed their time voluntarily for a cause they believed in.'
Ross Colquhoun, Director of National Collective (2011-2014)

'The referendum campaign was a democratic awakening for thousands of Scottish citizens..and it's fitting that this story of activism - and the sea of humanity it encompassed - is celebrated in IndyRef to ScotRef.'
Michael Gray, CommonSpace.Scot

978-1-86057-131-2   128pp   £14.99   PB

Scottish Political Parties and the 2014 Independence Referendum

Peter Lynch

Though the referendum saw the launch of umbrella campaign groups - Yes Scotland and Better Together - political parties remained central to the campaign. This study:
- analyses the referendum roles and activities of the Conservatives, Scottish Greens, Labour, Liberal Democrats, the SNP and the Scottish Socialist Party during the campaign.
- places the independence referendum in international context by examining other sovereignty referendums
- looks at the emergence of new organisations like Radical Independence and National Collective.

978-1-86057-121-3   172pp   £24.99   PB

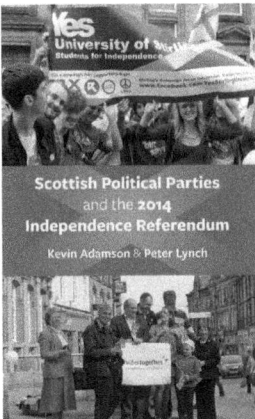

welsh academic press

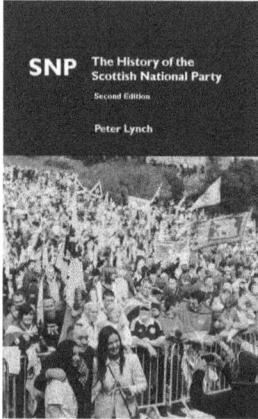

SNP
The History of the Scottish National Party
(Second Edition)

Peter Lynch

'lucid, comprehensive and balanced - an invaluable guide to the SNP'
David Torrance

'There is scholarship on every page. It will become the definitive reference work on the nationalist strand of Scottish politics and Scottish history...the early days in particular are extremely well done, with close attention to original sources... impressive and has never been so well set out before.'
Scottish Affairs

The first full-length history of the Scottish National Party which traces the fortunes of the SNP from its establishment in 1934 to winning power in the Scottish Parliament.

978-1-86057-057-5   319pp   £19.99   PB

The Public Affairs Guide to
Scotland

Robert McGeachy & Mark Ballard

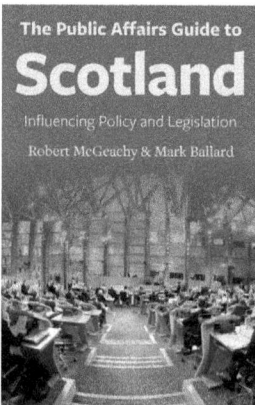

'I've worked in Scottish public affairs for many years but this book is still a great resource for clear guidance, ideas and planning. We keep one in our office and refer to it often. Colleagues new to the field of public affairs describe it as invaluable.'
Kim Hartley, Head, Royal Col. of Speech & Language Therapists Scotland

'Whether you need to engage with the legislative procedures of the Scottish Parliament and its policy development or hope to inform the development of a Bill, this book provides in depth help.'
Satwat Rehman, Director, One Parent Families Scotland

'Both authors have used their tremendous experience to really good effect. I really can't praise their efforts highly enough.'
Bill Scott, Policy Director, Inclusion Scotland

'...contains all a person needs to know to engage with the Parliament, the Government, local authorities and civic society in an effective and efficient way.'
Michael P Clancy OBE

'Mark Ballard and Robert McGeachy, through the pages of this important book, are ... doing democracy a service.'
Michael Russell, MSP for Argyll & Bute

978-1-86057-126-8   224pp   £19.99   PB

Lightning Source UK Ltd.
Milton Keynes UK
UKHW020037221119
353974UK00005B/395/P